# The Politics of Community Services

**Network Foundation for Educational Publishing**
is a voluntary foundation set up:

1. To facilitate the development of a healthy and responsible Canadian-controlled post-secondary book publishing sector.
2. To assist in the production, dissemination and popularizing of innovative texts and other educational materials for people at all levels of learning.
3. To develop more varied sources for critical works in the Humanities and Social Sciences.
4. To expand the readership for Canadian academic works beyond a select body of scholars.
5. To encourage the academic community to create books on Canadian topics for the community at large.
6. To develop works that will contribute to public information and debate on issues of historical and contemporary concern, thereby improving standards of education and public participation.

**The Network Basics Series,** one of the Foundation's activities, provides inexpensive books on the leading edge of research and debate to students and the general public.

This Network Basic is published by Garamond Press. Please direct all enquiries to 67A Portland Street, Toronto, Ontario, M5V 2M9.

# The Politics of Community Services

## Immigrant Women, Class and State

*Roxana Ng*

*Garamond Press*
*Toronto, Ont.*

A Publication of Garamond Press

Garamond Press
67A Portland Street
Toronto, Ontario M5V 2M9

Cover design: Sharon Nelson
Typesetting: LaserGraphics, Halifax
Printed and bound in Canada

We gratefully acknowledge the Department of the Secretary of State for financial assistance in the production of this book.

**Canadian Cataloguing in Publication Data**

Ng, Roxana, 1951-
The politics of community services

(Network basics series)
Bibliography: p. 107
ISBN 0-920059-42-2

1. Employment agencies - Political aspects. 2. Women immigrants - employment. 3. Labor policy
I. Title. II. Series

HD5861.N4 1987 331.12'8 C87-094716-8

# Contents

# Diagrams

# Dedication

This book is dedicated to the memory of my grandmother, Dr. F.S. Tseng, and my godmother, Mrs. Y.D. So, both casualties of the immigration process.

## Acknowledgements

Many people have contributed to the completion of this book. In addition to the people I acknowledged in my thesis, I wish to once again register my intellectual indebtedness to Dorothy E. Smith, whose work has both instructed and inspired my own. Since completing my thesis, I have continued to learn from and be challenged by friends who are active in different kinds of organizing efforts: Pramila Aggarwal, Valerie Bezanson, Kari Delhi, Alice deWolffe, Becky George, and Susan Heald. Anka Broch-due, Nancy Jackson, Marie Graff, Bill Berinati, and Sylvia Jong looked after me, especially during the critical time when I moved from one province to another. Marilee Reimer provided the bridge for this transition. Jake Muller remains, as always, my most ardent critic and support. Finally, I want to thank the people at Garamond Press, especially Errol Sharpe, who made this project into a reality.

Roxana Ng
Fredericton, N.B.
January 1988

Chapter One

# Immigrant Women, Community Work, and Class Relations

## Introduction

When I began this study in 1980, it was to be an investigation of immigrant women in the paid labour force. Specifically, I wanted to investigate *how* immigrant women were organized into the positions they occupied in the labour market hierarchy (cf. Boyd, 1975, 1986; Arnopoulos, 1979; Jenke and Yaron, 1979). It ended as an analysis of the internal transformation of a community employment agency for immigrant women. As well, through observing the counsellors' daily work of job counselling and placement, I came to see how "immigrant women" were *produced* as a labour market category. In other words, I saw how class relations were reproduced in the ordinary activities of daily life. Thus, it can be said that this book captures a moment in the production and reproduction of class in Canadian society.

After finishing a study on immigrant housewives in 1980 (Ng and Ramirez, 1981), I decided to conduct a parallel study on women's situations in the labour force. The employment agency recommended to me, by a number of activists in the immigrant community, was a group which was successful in helping women to find employment and in securing government funding at a time when overall government spending on community groups had been reduced.

The employment agency was a voluntary non-profit organization, registered under the Incorporation Act, which provided job counselling and placement services for non-English speaking and black women. It was established by activists in the immigrant community of a metropolitan city in Ontario, who were dissatisfied with existing services by other organizations. They rallied community support, and lobbied the state to provide funding to set up the agency, which had a clear advocacy role. That is, the agency claimed to work in the interest of immigrant women and help them overcome barriers in the labour market. In so doing, members of the agency also intended to improve the overall status of immigrant women in the labour force.

At the time of my research, the employment agency was funded through the Outreach Program of the federal Department of Employment and Immigration (EIC). By examining the work process of the agency in terms of state and labour market relations, I discovered that the agency's operation underwent certain transformations from its inception, so that it came to function on behalf of the state apparatus in organizing and producing immigrant women as a distinctive kind of labour, as "commodities," in the Canadian labour market.

As a result of its funding arrangement, the employment agency now entered into a sub-contractual relationship with the state. The funding protocol was such that the agency had to produce a "product" for the state in return for funding. The nature and parameter of this "product" was defined by a legal contract, signed by the board of directors, who were legally accountable to the state and "the public" for the agency's financial welfare. As such, they became the internal representatives of the state within the agency.

This "product" was given visibility and definition through an elaborate accounting system which was to be executed by the agency staff. The requirements of the funding program, as well as the expanded capacity of the agency, led to an internal fragmentation of the work process within the agency itself. This in turn led to certain tensions and contradictions inside the agency: tension between the board and the staff; tension between the "paperwork" and services to clients (immigrant women).

The "product" for which state funding was remunerated was defined, not so much in terms of advocacy, as in terms of services to *both* clients and employers, the buyers of the labour of immigrant women. The placement of women in job openings, therefore, progressively became a major consideration. In order for the agency to place women in jobs (ie. as the agency entered into labour market relations with employers), good relations with employers became paramount for the agency to secure a continual supply of job orders. This, to a certain extent, undermined the advocacy capacity of the agency, so that the work of the agency came to take on a contradictory character *vis-a-vis* immigrant women. In effect, the successful placement of clients depended upon conformity to employers' requirements for labour. In this way, the requirements for certain kinds of experiences and skills, the "quality" and "personality" of the clients, came to dominate the selection and matching process of immigrant women in relation to job openings. In the job counselling and placement process, then, what we will see is the production of immigrant women as "commodities" for employers, the buyers of these commodities. This process was partially accomplished through documents, which served to delineate and define the characteristics of these "commodities" specified by the "buyers."

In this way, the counselling and placement process was a moment in organizing the class locations of immigrant women in the Canadian social structure. The work of employment counsellors in "matching" immigrant women to available job openings, based on their marketable skills, work experiences, and the requirements of employers, was part of the process whereby a labour market stratified by gender and ethnicity was maintained and reproduced in a capitalist economy. Thus, the agency did not only organize, but actually helped rationalize, labour market processes on behalf of the state.

As I conducted fieldwork there, the tensions and contradictions which underlay the work processes of the agency became visible. After I had spent a certain period of time at the agency, it was difficult not to notice the frustration and exhaustion experienced by employment counsellors in their work. For example, while the agency's goal was to place immigrant women in the best possible job openings with some degree of upward mobility, a consistent feature was that clients of the agency ended up in minimum wage, assembly-line jobs or as restaurant and domestic help. Unless a client had a high level of command of English and officially recognized educational credentials, it was almost impossible to enrol her in a skill-upgrading or job-training program. In this regard, attempting to obtain government subsidies for clients, who were mostly "sponsored immigrants" (see next section), to take basic English language training was a constant struggle between the counsellors and Employment and Immigration personnel.

Although funding from the Outreach program had enabled the agency to expand its services, the agency also experienced a concommitant increase in client in-take because of increasing demand. On the day-to-day level, there was a persistent tension between the provision of services to clients, and the rising demand for producing documentary materials, from time sheets recording the counsellors' working hours to statistical and case records on clients, not to mention bookkeeping and other financial records.

When the workload became impossible to manage, one way of coping, for the counsellors, was to close the agency's door for a day or an afternoon and refuse to admit clients. Occasionally, instead of giving clients extended counselling sessions, the counsellor would make a placement as quickly as possible. When, initially, the counsellor had attempted to act as an advocate for her clients, as time went on, she began to adopt an "objective" and non-committal stance in client-employer disputes so as not to offend employers. In her daily work, the counsellor constantly had to strike a balance between her role as an advocate and her relationship with government officials and employers on whom the agency depended for funding and for a continual supply of job orders.

In terms of its structure, there was increasing animosity between board and staff members over decision-making affecting the operation of the agency. The agency was caught in the dilemma of striving toward a more-or-less egalitarian mode of operation and an emerging hierarchy resulting from the incorporation and funding procedures. The various funding crises had created and deepened the division between paid staff and volunteers in their role as board members, who had previously worked cooperatively to further the well-being of the agency. The tensions underpinning these changes were experienced by the agency as a series of never-ending crises, which the staff, as well as the board, had to deal with on a continual basis.

This book is an investigation into the way in which the employment agency was organized by state and labour market processes so that its services came to have this contradictory character *vis-a-vis* the interest of immigrant women. In so doing, it illuminates how class rule is accomplished as an ongoing practice in people's activities in the everyday world: as people go about looking for work and as they go about doing their jobs. Through this analysis, we see that class is not merely a theoretical category; nor can it be reduced to a set of occupational and economic indicators. It is a *process* which is enacted and re-enacted by people's daily activities in securing their livelihood.

The remainder of this chapter will discuss the usage of the term, "immigrant women," and the theoretical and methodological procedures employed for the study. Chapter 2 traces the history of the employment agency in its political context. Chapters 3 and 4 describe the funding and counselling processes, respectively. Chapter 5 provides an overview of the effects of the processes described in Chapters 3 and 4. To conclude, Chapter 6 explores the possibilities and limits of community work in light of the analysis undertaken.

## The Social Construction of Immigrant Women

Technically, the term, "immigrant women," refers to women who are landed immigrants in Canada. Using this definition, many researchers found that these women tended to concentrate at the top and bottom of the occupational hierarchy, either in skilled professional jobs or in non-skilled and dead-end positions (eg. Boyd, 1975, 1986; Arnopoulos, 1978). In everyday life, however, women who are white, educated, and English-speaking are rarely considered to be immigrant women.

The term conjures up the image of a woman who does not speak English or who speaks English with an accent; who is from the Third World or a member of a visible minority group; and who has a certain type of job (eg. a sewing machine operator or a cleaning lady). Thus, "immigrant women" is a socially constructed category presupposing, among other things, a labour market relation.

Women who are considered to be immigrants in Canada have not always been so considered. They *become* immigrant women when they immigrate to Canada and enter certain positions in the labour market. Thus, when we call someone an "immigrant woman" we are in fact naming a process whereby this individual comes to be identified as an immigrant woman.

In this book, I will adopt the common sense usage of the term "immigrant women." My purpose is to discover *how* some women *become* immigrant women in Canadian society. What we will see is that the work of employment counsellors is one "moment" in the social construction of immigrant women as the employment agency entered into relations with the state and with employers.

Historically, immigrant women are the product of capitalist development, which displaces segments of the population from their indigenous livelihood and draws them to centres of new industrial development. There, they are more and more tied to an economy based on profit making: a monetary economy. Immigrant women become a social entity after the rise of the phenomenon of immigration, which in turn indicates a process whereby different labour supply systems are integrated into the world capitalist economy (see Sassen-Koob, 1981).

In Canada, immigrant women become a visible social category when female labour is employed in large numbers, such as in the latter half of the nineteenth century when England experienced a surplus of single, unemployed women whereas the colonies, including Canada and Australia, were in need of domestic labour and wives (see Lay, 1980), and more recently when male immigrants were allowed to bring their families into Canada as permanent residents. In the 1970s, this pattern of female immigration coincided with the downturn of the Canadian economy when the quota for "independent immigrants" was cut down and the policy of "family reunification" was stressed.

The Canadian state plays a crucial role in determining the position of immigrant women through the Immigration Act. Immigration policies have always been designed to meet and regulate the needs of the Canadian economy while, as much as possible, preserving Canada as a predominantly white nation (see Avery, 1979, Basran, 1983). The current Act, which came into effect in 1978, seems fairly straight forward at first glance. It divides immigrants into three categories: independent immigrants, including "assisted relatives," whose entry into Canada is subject to economic requirements and criteria measured by a point system; "sponsored" or "family class" immigrants, who do not accrue enough points by themselves and who are sponsored into Canada by a close relative; and business-class immigrants who have capital to invest in Canadian industries and businesses. In addition, immigrants can apply for refugee status, and be assessed by a different set of criteria. The "family class" category is the one crucial to our discussion.

This classification of immigrants, as such, does not distinguish between the gender, ethnic origin, or class position of individuals. But when we take into account the indexes for determining entry of "independent immigrants" (based on language proficiency, educational attainment, investment potential, and the labour requirements of Canada, ranked according to a point system), then the sexist, racist and class biases of the immigration policy become visible.

The majority of the people entering Canada as "sponsored immigrants" are the elderly, children, and women from Third World or industrially less developed countries, who do not have the education, skills, and economic resources seen to be adequate for or relevant to the requirements of the Canadian economy. They are permitted to enter the country under the sponsorship of the man, seen to be the main wage-earner, or close relatives (eg. spouse, parents, adult children) already residing in Canada. Women, in particular, are frequently considered their husbands' dependants, and are classified as "family class," even when they have been working in the paid labour force in their home countries (see Estable, 1986). According to the philosophy of the policy, family class immigrants are to provide emotional and other support for the wage earner and are not destined for the labour market. In reality, due to financial necessity, many sponsored immigrants, especially the women, do engage in waged work (see Ng and Ramirez, 1981: esp.46-49).

These immigrant categories are not merely legal definitions. They have real social and economic consequences for people's lives. For example, a sponsored immigrant is not entitled to public assistance of any kind, such as training subsidies, welfare, etc., available to independent immigrants and other Canadians. They are seen to be the dependants of the sponsor, who is legally responsible for their financial welfare for a period of five to ten years (see Ng and Ramirez, 1981: 49-55; Ng and Das Gupta, 1981; Estable, 1986). They can be deported if they are deemed to be a financial burden to the Canadian state. This forces women to be completely dependent on their sponsor and contributes to their isolation and captivity in unpleasant and abusive family situations. The lack of access to government subsidized language- and job-training programs means that women are forced to seek jobs which are low paid and marginal.

Many factors in the labour market restrict immigrant women's occupational mobility: the segregated nature of the Canadian labour force (see Armstrong and Armstrong, 1981; Connelly, 1979); the lack of recognition of education, skills, and work experience from non-English and non-European countries; the lack of appropriate language and re-training programs (see IWS, 1985); pressures exerted by professional associations and labour unions to restrict membership (see Campbell, 1980; IWS, 1985), and so on.Thus, when they join the paid labour force, immigrant women are forced into certain labour pools at the lower end of the occupational hierarchy, frequently taking jobs that other Canadians would not take because of low wages and poor working conditions. Due to the nature of their paid employment (e.g.. part-time, seasonal, or piece work), labour standard legislation is not rigidly enforced in many cases, which further exacerbates the poor conditions of their work. Meanwhile, their domestic responsibilities, including childcare, and lack of educational opportunities mean that their mobility in the wage labour market is severely curtailed. As a result, most non-English speaking immigrant women, if they enter the labour force, become members of the most exploited sectors of the working population.[1]

This is the social context within which the work of the employment agency was situated. In order to improve the situation of immigrant women, employment counsellors had to enter into relations with employers and with the state, which ultimately curtailed their effectiveness. In our analysis, we will see how their work also played a part in the organization of immigrant women into an ethnic and gender segregated labour force, and contributed to determining their class positions.

## Framework and Method

The data, on which the analysis in this book is based, were obtained primarily from first-hand fieldwork at the employment agency from February to November, 1981. As already mentioned, I had gained access to the agency through contacts in the immigrant community.

The research strategy I adopted was participant observation. That is, I assisted the coordinator with compiling documentary materials as the need and demand arose. In return I could observe, unobtrusively, how the employment counsellors conducted their daily work. I was discouraged from interviewing the counsellors because of their heavy workload, and from interviewing clients for reasons of confidentiality.

My involvement in the agency changed over time. Initially, I worked closely with the coordinator. As I became more familiar with the other staff members and with the agency's operation, I took on other tasks, from answering the telephone to dealing with client inquiries. Finally, I began counselling clients.

Since I am fluent in Cantonese, one of the most common Chinese dialects spoken by Chinese immigrants in Canada, I naturally began working with the Chinese counsellor, and occasionally, took over the clients whom she couldn't handle due to her workload. At that time, immigrants from Southeast Asia (Chinese, Vietnamese, many of Chinese origin, and Cambodian) constituted the largest and increasing client group of the agency. With the constant changeover of staff throughout the summer and fall, at one point I became the most experienced Chinese counsellor, and was relied upon by the coordinator to train new counsellors. By getting involved in different aspects of the agency's work, I gained an encompassing picture of its total work process. When I began counselling, I was treated by others as a member of the staff. They began to include me in their conversations, answer any inquiries I posed, and teach me different ways of handling clients and employers. Thus, although I was not able to interview the staff formally, I gained an in-depth knowledge of them in their work.

In addition to this first-hand working knowledge, I had access to all of the agency's records, including funding proposals, correspondence with government personnel, statistical information, and official (i.e. public) records on clients and employers. I also interviewed two board members who were involved in setting up the agency, and got an overview of its history and development to supplement my fieldwork. As well, I visited the Ottawa Head Office and the Ontario Regional Office of the Outreach Program of the Department of Employment and Immigration. In Ottawa, I talked with the Outreach consultant responsible for the Ontario projects and the data analyst responsible for assessing the performance of the employment agency. At the Ontario regional office, I interviewed the director of the Outreach Program and the consultant responsible for the project. (For a summary of the different levels of responsibilities and authority, see Diagram 1.) All the officers I talked with in this government bureaucracy were very open about the history and politics of the Outreach Program itself, and their knowledge of the difficulties experienced by the employment agency.

To summarize, this analysis is based on three kinds of data. One, participant observation at the employment agency. Two, documentary materials including historical documents, statistical and case records kept by the agency, funding proposals, memoranda between the agency and Outreach, and Outreach manuals made available to me by the employment agency. Three, interviews conducted with members of the agency and Outreach bureaucrats at the regional and federal levels, which provided the context for locating the employment agency in a historical and political context.

***

To make sense of the tensions and contradictions I witnessed at the employment agency, I followed a line of inquiry in sociology adapted from Marx's method of political economy (Sayer, 1979; Smith, 1981b, 1981c). This approach has been called "institutional ethnography" by Smith (1981c). Unlike standard ethnographic research, which describes a local setting as if it was a self-contained unit of analysis, institutional ethnography seeks to locate the dynamics of a local setting in the complex institutional relations organizing the local dynamics.

In terms of my study, the employment agency was taken to be one component of a larger work process in the highly complex division of labour characteristic of an advanced capitalist social formation; the interactions within the agency could not be understood without reference to the organizational context within which it was situated. Thus, in addition to recording the routine daily work of employment counsellors, I paid particular attention to the historical development of the agency and its linkages to other organizations and relations. My own participation in the agency and my increasing competence as a counsellor was central to my subsequent analysis of the workings of the employment agency. It was through participating as a competent member of the setting that I was able to acquire an understanding of the institutional processes to which the agency was linked.

What came into view, when I adopted this approach, was that the act of counselling did not begin or end in the agency. It was connected to a set of social relations which had to do with the way in which the state attempted to regulate and rationalize labour market demands through contracting out some of its functions to community groups with closer ties to the grassroots. The counselling and placement process thus constituted one component in a set of social actions which organized the relation between immigrant women and employers in the labour market.

Once we develop this understanding and grasp this set of connections, we then see that although the counsellor's individual "style" might be idiosyncratic, the relations underpinning that activity were not. They (the social relations of the labour market) could not be reduced to a simple set of transactions. The agency was also shaped by its relationship to the state. The funding procedures which organized its operation were not peculiar to this agency. They had been elaborated over time as the *general* forms of such relations. To fulfill the agency's funding obligations to the state, the counsellors necessarily entered their work into this social course of action which gave the counselling process its determinate character. This had very little to do with the intention of the counsellors *vis-a-vis* their clients. Thus, my analysis of the counselling process must not be construed as a critique of the counsellors' style. It is intended to illuminate the labour market relations to which the counselling process was inevitably tied, which are at the same time the class relations of contemporary capitalist societies.

Obviously, this concept of class deviates from its standard treatment in stratification theory, which measures class in terms of economic and social indicators (eg. income, merit, social background). My understanding follows a recent revival in Marxist analyses which focus on class as a set of social relations: relations between people (see Sayer, 1979; Smith, 1983; Cockburn, 1983).

Marx and Engels, in *The German Ideology* (1970) and *The Communist Manifesto* (1967), view all forms of societies and change in society as arising out of the struggles between different groups/classes of people in terms of their relation to the means of production. In capitalist societies, the two major classes are the bourgeoisie (or capitalists), who own and control the means of production, and the proletariat (the working class), who must sell their labour power in exchange for a wage because they do not own the means of production. However, Marx and Engels hasten to add that these classes are not homogeneous apart from this broadest definition of their respective relationship to the means of production. Each class emerges and is given cohesion and definition in relation to the other; it is also internally fragmented. This is what they say of wage labour: "Wage labour rests exclusively on competition between labourers" (Marx and Engels, 1967: 93).

Furthermore, the exploitation of the labourers by the capitalists is not a simple, one-way relation. It is a contradictory process. In bringing workers together into a factory to maximize the generation and augmentation of production for capital, and educating workers to use new machinery and equipment (albeit for the purpose of eliminating some workers to cut costs in the long run), the bourgeoisie also brings workers together, revealing their common conditions of exploitation. This process in fact facilitates the formation of the proletariat as a class (Marx and Engels, 1967; Marx, 1954). Thus, the concept of "class" is not just a delineation of a set of social and economic indicators. It is fundamentally a relation between two groups of people (albeit internally fragmented) who are engaged in a process of mutual definition and re-definition over time (Marx and Engels, 1967; Thompson, 1963; Cockburn, 1983).

Contemporary theorists, Smith in particular, draw attention to class relations as practical activities. That is, in order for class to be an objective feature of contemporary societies, it must be *accomplished* by people (see Smith, 1981; 1983). In her investigation of women and class, Smith examines the activities of bourgeois women in organizing the transgenerational relations of the bourgeoisie, and the fragmentation of gender (women in her case) along class lines (Smith, 1983). Dehli's study of home-school relations in early twentieth-century Toronto shows the dominant role played by upper middle class mothers in developing "proper mothering practices" which were antithetical to the interests of working class (immigrant) women (Dehli, 1984).

My analysis follows this tradition in Marxist thought and develops the notion of class as a set of practices which organize relations among people. This book focusses on the practices of employment counsellors in organizing immigrant women's relation to the paid labour force, and the organization of the internal relations of the employment agency. These changing relations will be described to throw light on how class is created by a set of routine activities in everyday life.

Central to the (re)organization of class relations in contemporary societies is the state. In advanced capitalist societies, "the state" has increasingly taken on the role of mediating and intervening in the economy, augmenting the infrastructure essential for the continuous accumulation of capital. It actively organizes and manages the economy and the work force through special grants and tax shelters to businesses and industries, monitoring the work force by developing educational and training programs, and facilitating and regulating labour supply through legislation, including immigration policy and unemployment insurance. In this way, the state plays a major part in the constitution and organization of the working class through various intervention and control mechanisms.

The progressive expansion of the functions of the state and its formal organization is the central debate in Marxist scholarship.[2] This book does not take up this debate directly. Instead, it makes use of a more general understanding of the state (see, for example, Miliband, 1969; Poulantzas, 1978, 1980; Therborn, 1980; Corrigan and Sayer, 1985; London-Edinburgh Weekend Return Group, 1979). Simply put, the state is not a monolithic structure, composed of different apparatuses, which perform different functions for the dominant classes on behalf of capital. It is also the focus and embodiment of struggles between classes. My purpose is to discover "how the state in concrete ways organizes the hegemony of dominant classes" (Findlay, 1982:14); or, put in another way, "what does the ruling class do when it rules?" (Therborn, 1980). In order not to distract the reader from the empirical examination of the workings of the state, I will use the common sense usage of the term as short-hand to refer to the multiplicity of levels, functions, and activities of the government. At the end of the book, I will re-examine this usage, to see whether in fact it is adequate in accounting for the relations analysed.

One central aspect of ruling and the coordination of the complex functions of the state are documents. Documents, in various shapes and forms, provide for organizational action in the state apparatus and other large bureaucratic organizations: in records and files, legislation, press releases, orders-in-council, memoranda, and various kinds of informationn systems (see Garfinkel, 1967; Wheeler, 1969; Smith, 1974, 1984; Jackson, 1980; Campbell, 1984). The documentary process is crucial for organizing the complex division of labour within the state and ensuring its reproduction, because people move in and out of, and have a limited "life-span" relative to this structure. It is through documents of various kinds, from interdepartmental memoranda to job descriptions to statistical data, that the multitude of the seemingly disparate activities of the state apparatus is coordinated and given coherence. This documentary mode of action concretizes and binds departments and individuals to a legal course of action.

Indeed, through this process, the employment agency became connected to the state apparatus, although in appearance it remained an independent community agency. My study shows that in actual fact its functions were an extension of the coordinated activities of the state. As we will see in Chapter 5, it was through documents that employment counsellors organized and produced groups of women (in this case immigrant women) as particular kinds of workers (particular "commodities") for the labour market.

***

I want to devote a few words to the way in which the contradictions and tensions observed in the fieldwork process are handled in the study. As Cockburn has pointed out, "[i]f sociology has found it difficult to take account of contradiction, in real life people are only too painfully aware of it" (Cockburn, 1983: 11). Certainly, it was not easy for the people I studied to confront the tensions and contradictions which saturated the interactions at the agency. During my fieldwork, I saw how the counsellors were pained and baffled by their own inconsistency in dealing with clients, especially when they had to justify their action (or so they felt) to a researcher who detachedly looked on. Personally, I had to face the increasing tension I myself experienced being a researcher and counsellor, as the antagonism among members of the agency deepened and my presence was no longer welcomed by the people with whom I had established a congenial working relationship. In analysing the data, however, I tried not to skirt around these features and treat them as "anomalies" to be put into residual categories apart from the "normal" routine of the agency. I treated them as inherent to its development and evolution. The assumption was that confronting these tensions and contradictions would tell us something about the internal dynamics of the agency (see Mao, 1967b). The question posed was: how was the agency socially organized so as to give rise to these contradictions and tensions? It was only when I seriously confronted these "anomalies" that I began to come to grips with the processes which shaped the life of the agency and which directed its work away from the intended goals of its founding members.

In telling the story of the agency, I use several devices to protect the identities of the agency and the individuals involved in the study. I have withheld the name of the agency and the city where it was located, and simply refer to it as "the employment agency." I have not attempted to make the province where the agency was anonymous, because many of the policies and guidelines I examined were within provincial jurisdiction. I identify the various officials in the EIC bureaucracy by their positions only. Given that the personnel in that department changed as often as that of the agency, those individuals occupying the positions are thereby accorded some degree of anonymity. Since the study's purpose was to pinpoint the social relations underpinning the counselling process and not to describe the individuals' performances and styles, I have not identified the counsellors. As well, they are not identified by the ethnic groups they served because their ethnic origins are not relevant to my analysis. I use pseudonyms randomly when referring to the individuals. In cases where the position of the individual is important to the context, I use the individual's title (eg. the coordinator). "The coordinator" refers to the individual holding that position at the time, and not necessarily to only one person. Since different people filled this position at various times, I hope this device protects their individual identity.

For people familiar with the immigrant community, however, these devices may not be completely adequate to guarantee the subjects' anonymity. When reading this book, the reader should bear in mind that what are being described and analysed here are the social processes which underpinned the life of the employment agency and not the performances or character of individual members. As I already mentioned, individual members' intentions have little to do with the social course of action into which their activities enter.

By documenting and analysing the struggles of the employment agency, I hope that this book will contribute, in a small way, to the emerging analyses of progressive community and social movements in the English-speaking world (e.g. Morgan, 1981; London-Edinburgh Weekend Return Group, 1979; Piven and Cloward, 1977). As Cockburn, in her study on the transformation of the printing trade in England, correctly points out,

> ... it is precisely out of the process of bringing such contradictions to consciousness and facing up to illogicality or inconsistency, that a person takes a grip on his or her own fate. Politically it is of vital importance that we understand how we change (Cockburn, 1983: 13).

It is in this framework that I put forward my analysis.

Chapter Two

# History and Development of the Employment Agency

## The Politics of Citizen Participation

In many ways, the birth and evolution of the employment agency foreshadowed the tensions and contradictions I observed there. Its structural transformation, resulting from the incorporation procedures for funding purposes, illuminates the progressive penetration of the state into grassroots community activities since the mid-sixties under the rubric of "citizen participation."

Of course, the involvement of the voluntary sector in the welfare of immigrants is not a new phenomenon. Historically, philanthropic organizations, notably those organized by upper middle class women, were active in managing the emigration and welfare of working class single women and girls from Britain to Canada (Roberts, 1980; Lay, 1980). While immigration matters were the domain of upper class women in the late nineteenth century, as the Canadian state expanded its management function, it gradually began regulating immigration. In her research on the immigration work of these ladies, Roberts observed that, by the 1920s, immigration reform and the management of the ladies' organizations (through funding), had come under the jurisdiction of the state (Roberts, 1978; 1980).

While upper middle class women continued to play an important part in voluntary charitable activities, the mushrooming of the voluntary sector in contemporary times was in response to a different set of social and economic circumstances. Since the sixties, members of the intelligentsia, many of whom are young people, became increasingly active in community work. Whereas upper class women from the earlier period saw their role as one of nation building, those involved in community work in the more recent period aimed at transforming the social structure and redistributing the existing wealth and resources by organizing the disadvantaged sectors of the population.

Although the history of community work in Canada since the 60s is not well documented, we see many parallel developments of its counterparts in Britain and the United States. Its proliferation was prompted by the rediscovery of poverty and inequality after the post-war boom (Edwards and Batley, 1978). In both the US and Britain, it was discovered that class, sex, location, and home environment were important variables in the persistence of inequality (Edwards and Batley, 1978: 15-21).

In Canada, deteriorating economic conditions in Quebec led to increasing radicalism and militancy in that province. The separatist movement gathered momentum both among the militant Left and the Right (Milner and Milner, 1973). This was accompanied by the rising militancy of Francophone communities across Canada that demanded language and cultural rights (see Denis and Li, 1983). As well, Canada experienced a growing influx of immigrants from Europe and the Third World with the liberalization of immigration policy in 1947. The concentration of immigrants—many of whom were from visible minorities and non-British backgrounds—in urban centres led to new problems of settlement and racial tension in many cities. In this social climate, the myth of social and racial equality within the Canadian "mosaic" (Porter 1967) could no longer be maintained. In addition, other disadvantaged groups, such as tenants, unemployed youths, and women, were also awakening to their predicament in this hierarchy.

Under these social and political circumstances, many policies and social programs, including the multiculturalism policy, were developed by the state to respond to the existing and potential problems of an increasingly fragmented society. These programs, couched in the rhetoric of "citizen participation," represented different ways to administer government funding to community groups for managing their own affairs and working out their own solutions to specific problems of their respective communities and constituencies.

While many analysts would argue that "citizen participation" was a form of social control (eg. Loney, 1977; Djao, 1983), I argue that it was a compromise arrived at by two opposing forces: the need to cope with changing social and economic reality by the state on the one hand, and the increasing militancy of minority groups and their advocates demanding social programs to meet their needs on the other. Given the nature of the capitalist state, how are capitalist social relations reproduced by community groups participating in these programs? Put a different way, how does state funding to these groups serve to dissipate potential dissension and maintain class domination?

In analysing the battered women's movement in the US, Morgan observed the expansion of what she called the state's "social problems apparatus" since the civil rights and anti-war movements of the 1960's (Morgan, 1981). While the specific ways in which the social problems apparatus diffused social and political struggle might be different in different situations, she identified three general processes which are applicable to my study: bureaucratization, individualization, and professionalization.

Bureaucratization and individualization fragment class issues through bureacratic structures by deflecting political demands into social ones. For example, the structural problems of the labour market faced by immigrant women are re-defined as *their* problem. Professionalization is the process which transforms non-capitalist forms of organization into hierarchical ones, as in the evolution of the employment agency from a collective structure into a bureaucratic and hierarchical one. Viewed in this light, state funding to community groups can be seen as an inexpensive alternative to a coercive approach and a way of defusing criticisms directed at the welfare state while meeting the growing demand for social programs. As we will see, through the processes outlined above, the conflicts and contradictions that arise from maintaining order are separated from the relations of production, which then become depoliticized (see Morgan, 1981), thus turning political and economic problems into "social" ones.

## The Outreach Program

Viewed in the context of "citizen participation," the Outreach Program of the federal Department of Employment and Immigration (EIC), was one way the state attempted to integrate marginalized groups into the labour market via the work of community organizations. Outreach was established by a cabinet decision as a short-term program within EIC. Its objective, according to various documents from Outreach, was

> To improve, with the help of community-based agencies, the employability and employment of individuals who experience special difficulties competing in the labour market and who are not able to benefit effectively from the services offered by their CEC (Canada Employment Centres). The essential purpose of Outreach

is to complement, and effectively extend, regular services of the Commission to such groups.

Under this general objective, several groups were chosen to be under the jurisdiction of the Outreach Program. These were:

a) Residents of isolated or remote communities;
b) Native Peoples;
c) Chronically unemployed, usually welfare recipients;
d) Mentally or physically handicapped persons;
e) Inmates and ex-inmates;
f) Persons who experience great difficulty in labour force entry or re-entry.

Provisions were made within the guidelines to allow for changes in target groups according to changing labour market needs and social conditions. Thus, women and youth "who fall within the above groups" were added to this targetted population. The Program was administered locally through regional offices that were mandated to develop regional policies and local priorities in relation to the supply and demand of local labour markets, including determining their own target groups.

When the Program was established in 1972, it was to be on a short-term and experimental basis. Community groups were encouraged to design projects which would enable EIC to identify special needs clients and resolve the particular problem(s) of their employability. At that time, officials responsible for the Program did not foresee its survival beyond ten years.

However, once funding was made available to community groups, as one official reflected, it was not so easy to withhold it later. A myriad of community groups fought for their own survival through Outreach. They mobilized their constituencies, their respective communities, politicians, and the media in order to obtain funding. When politicians became involved and the Minister personally contacted by the electorate, sometimes "special cases" were granted, and hence the Program was never phased out by the original deadline.

In 1975, the emphasis of Outreach shifted to the direct delivery of services by projects themselves. In 1979, following a drastic cut in its overall 1978-79 budget, the Program was again under review. Among the changes proposed by the Executive Director of Employment and Insurance in 1981, an effort was made to re-emphasize the temporary nature of projects with annual renewals; the maximum term of a project was set at four years. Again, this was met with negative and vocal reactions from recipient groups, as indicated by the summary of the consultative meeting held by Outreach with community groups in June, 1981.

It is clear, from the available information, that the Outreach Program was designed to tap those marginalized sectors of the labouring population (eg. Native people, the physically and mentally handicapped) whom the Canada Employment Centres failed to reach effectively. Traditionally, recruitment of these workers relied on informal contacts and networks, such as by word-of-mouth and "walk-in." With increasing unemployment and more previously so-called "secondary" workers joining the work force (eg. women, youths, and senior citizens), however, these recruitment methods became less and less satisfactory. Employers were not always able to recruit reliable workers; workers did not necessarily have the appropriate contacts to identify suitable employment. In this regard, we see the state stepping in to take an active part in organizing these workers in relation to their employers by creating a funding program, Outreach.

In doing so, the state accomplished two things. First, as its name indicates, the Outreach Program enabled the state to extend itself into and organize the labour force at the grassroots level without adding a great deal to the costly expansion of the bureaucracy. Second, through the provision of funding to community groups, it entered into a contractual relationship with these groups, thereby bringing them to a cooperative, instead of a confrontative, stance *vis-a-vis* the state. The emphasis of this cooperative relationship was stated clearly in a public information document of the Program made available to community groups:

> What is the relationship of Outreach projects with the Canada Employment Centre (Manpower) services?
>
> Outreach projects work in close cooperation with Manpower offices to better serve their clients, using commission services and programs such as testing and training. Manpower staff offers guidance and expertise to project sponsors when the need arises and keeps sponsors informed of all services available for Outreach clients. In return, commission employees can significantly improve their expertise in dealing with these clients by observing the techniques pioneered by Outreach staff (i.e. people working in the community organizations).

What we see here is that pressures from below for the state to improve the conditions of the marginal work force was transformed into "services" through the funding program. The structural problems inherent in a capitalist labour market with a constantly expanding surplus population were translated into the problems of the targetted population, and were subsumed under the rubric, "client need."[1] In this way, the work of community groups with "clients" was severed from its political and economic context. It was turned into a definable "product" (a set of services) specified by the Program via a contractual agreement. The parameters of the activities which could be undertaken by the groups, now translated into "services" to clients, were thus circumscribed.

## History of the Employment Agency

In describing the development of the agency, it is important to bear in mind that its history, obtained primarily from interviews with staff and board members who were involved with the agency from an earlier phase, was a reconstruction based on the interviewees' memories and interpretations of "what actually happened." From the interviews, many discrepancies of "facts" emerged. The purpose of the present account is not to determine and record the correct "facts," but to illuminate the internal tensions which characterized the development of the agency from its inception. From this account, we not only get a sense of the development of the agency, first as a project[2] sponsored by another organization, but also its interactional dynamics leading up to the time of my fieldwork.

The employment agency began around 1977, as a breakaway from another employment agency servicing immigrant women after internal disputes. When this occurred, the staff of the original employment agency contacted several organizations and individuals in the immigrant community about their plight. With the help of two organizations, the staff began their own project under the sponsorship of one of the organizations, and submitted a funding proposal to Canada Works (another EIC funding program).

By the time the project was approved in January, 1978, however, the applicants had found other jobs, and the organization under which the application was made did not want to administer the project. An advisory committee, composed of representatives of the two sponsoring organizations, members of the breakaway group, and other interested individuals involved in the immigrant community, was struck to oversee the project in a voluntary capacity.

Four staff members were hired to execute the project: three counsellors servicing West Indian, Italian, and Chinese clients, and a public relations officer (who later became the Spanish counsellor when clients from that language group increased). At first, the Chinese counsellor assumed the position of the coordinator and received a higher wage for her administrative responsibilities, which were fairly straightforward under the Canada Works Program. Since the staff had no previous employment counselling experience, they intially worked closely with the advisory committee. As they gained experience and as the project became more successful, they moved away from the committee, and worked as an autonomous team.

From the beginning, disagreements about the goals and directions of the project emerged within the advisory committee. Some argued that it should be oriented toward job readiness; others maintained that the immediate need for job counselling and placement was paramount. In the end, a compromise was reached where job placement was carried out as a major activity on an experimental basis, but other services, such as counselling and job readiness, were also seen as essential components of the project. There was also disagreement as to whether the project should continue after the Canada Works grant, which was for a 12-month period. While the staff was in favour of its continuation, some members of the advisory committee were against it, with the result that those opposed resigned from the committee.

Several major events marked the end of the first year of the project's operation. Firstly, due to its success, at the end of the 12-month funding period the project was granted a 6-month extension by Canada Works to enable the project to seek more permanent funding. Secondly, since the sponsoring organization did not wish to be responsible for the project, the the coordinator was asked by the Canada Works project officer to act as its interim sponsor. The understanding was that in the long run, the project would begin the incorporation process and become a non-profit charitable organization.

Thirdly, as a result of the unstable funding situation, some staff members, including the coordinator, quit. As a result of discussions among the staff, the Italian counsellor became the *de facto* coordinator. To maintain the egalitarian mode of working and to encourage a team spirit during a time when the morale of the project was low, the Italian counsellor agreed to split the extra portion of her salary with the other staff members. This later became a contentious issue when this coordinator left, because it was an unofficial arrangement not recognized by either the board (who came into existence after the project was incorporated) or the funding program (Outreach).

In the spring and summer of 1979, the project launched an extensive fundraising drive to secure permanent funding. Efforts were focussed on the EIC since most provincial and private sources indicated that employment was a federal responsibility. But no promise of funding was forthcoming. A "Summer Swan Song" was planned as a dramatic closing of the project. In the words of the coordinator, this event was "to communicate to the community that the agency was closing and the reasons for its closing." To this end, in addition to members of the "community" (which included clients and community workers), politicians from the three levels of government, as well as the media, were contacted. It was a successful effort. The plight of the project received national coverage in the media, and the Minister of Employment and Immigration communicated to the project that he would meet with its representatives. After the meeting, a special grant was made available to the project from the Minister's emergency fund to enable the project to continue to the end of March, 1980, at which time it would be eligible for funding available through the Outreach Program.

## The Incorporation Process

Viewed in light of the politics of citizen participation, the incorporation process is another extension of the state's ruling capacity into community activities. The effects of the incorporation process on the internal relations of the employment agency will be discussed in Chapter 5. Here, we will trace the development of the agency up to its incorporation and discuss the concommitant changes resulting from it.

Several developments prompted the decision of the project to incorporate itself. Firstly, as already discussed, if it was to continue, it had to become an independent organization because the sponsoring organization was unwilling to be responsible for it. Secondly, although incorporation was not an official requirement for obtaining funding from EIC, the Canada Works project officer advised the project to become incorporated; incorporated groups were viewed more favourably by funding sources due to its legal structure of accountability. This proved to be correct as the project began its fundraising drive. All sources approached, from the United Way to private foundations, required that the project be an incorporated group.

There were two major consequences of the incorporation process. First, it narrowed the mandate of the project, now a full-fledged employment agency. During the title search, the first step in the incorporation procedures through the Dept. of Corporate and Consumers' Affairs, the project was told that its name was too broad. Eventually, the title specifically referring to placement services was approved. As we will see, despite the fact that members of the agency frequently argued its unique role in providing employment services for immigrant women, ultimately the placement function was what the agency was mandated and funded to do.

Second, the incorporation process introduced a formal and legally binding structure of accountability into the agency. The newly incorporated agency consisted of a board of directors, paid staff, and the membership. Whereas the advisory committee was an informal body with no official power, the board of directors were the legal "managers" of the agency, accountable to the funding body and the membership for its financial health. Under this new structure, the staff, who previously had the sole responsibility of overseeing the entire operation and policy development of the agency, became the "hired hands." Staff members were not so much accountable to the clients and community served by the agency, as to the board of directors, who had the official power to hire and fire staff. In this way, the board of directors became the internal representatives of the state *vis-a-vis* the staff.

In addition, the role of the coordinator was formalized, at least on paper. She became the "supervisor" of the staff and the intermediary between the staff and the board, directly accountable to the board and responsible for reporting to the board the success or failure of the agency to meet its mandate. Indeed, the board's knowledge of the operation of the agency was mediated by the coordinator. Although both the staff and the board tried very hard, at least initially, to preserve the previously egalitarian structure of the agency, in the final analysis, a hierarchy had been introduced. This development created an irreversible rift in the internal relations of the agency.

The final component in this new composition was the membership, which, at the time of my research, was a rather amorphous and undefined group. Since the agency did not really have a membership at the time of incorporation, board members were selected from the advisory committee and the immigrant community by the staff. As we will see, the legality of the board was called into question when conflicts arose within the agency, which had their origin in this earlier history of the group.

***

When I began my fieldwork at the agency, it was operating under the structure I described above, with a board of directors and four paid staff, one of whom was the coordinator. It was at the end of its first year of operation under the Outreach Program, and in the process of negotiating funding with Outreach for another fiscal year. The funding situation, similar to the transition period described earlier, was at best unstable, producing a lot of tension in the daily work environment. Due to the funding crisis, the board was becoming increasingly involved with the financial side of the agency, which in turn created tension in the board-staff interactions. This tension was interpreted as personal and ideological differences by members of the agency. However, my analysis indicates that it grew out of the incorporation and funding processes, which structured the internal relationships among the members. These relations will be explicated in Chapters 3 and 5.

Chapter Three

# The Funding Process

## The Sub-contractual Relationship between the Employment Agency and the State

Seen within the framework of the politics of citizen participation, the Outreach Program was a rather innovative form of extra-bureaucratic organization which enabled the state to extend into and regulate grass-roots activities at relatively low cost. Although it is true that the employment agency had always been funded by state programs, these programs varied a great deal and they imposed different conditions and requirements on the recipient organizations. As a make-work program, the Canada Works Program was geared toward providing "youths" with work experience. The administrative demands made on the recipient project was relatively low. By contrast, projects funded under the Outreach Program were considered an arm of the state bureaucracy. This relationship was clearly spelt out in the contractual agreements between the groups funded and Outreach.

Community groups funded by Outreach were required to work in cooperation with Canada Employment Centres (CECS) in their respective localities, servicing the client groups which the CECS currently had limited or no capacity to service. Mutual referral of clientele between Outreach projects and CECS was meant to be a routine matter. This relation between various EIC departments and Outreach projects was clearly indicated by the contracts between Outreach and its projects, and the assessment of projects. The following excerpt from an Outreach document is an example.

> A primary assessment factor will be the manner in which the project relates to the CMC/CEC, viz. the extent to which the project:
> i) complements and/or extends the services of the CMC/CEC;
> ii) utilizes CMC/CEC, programs and services;
> iii) meets agreed upon CMC/CEC project goals and objectives, including the development of a plan of action to eventually integrate the Outreach clientele into the mainline delivery system.[1]

In applying for funding from Outreach, therefore, the employment agency entered into a contractual agreement with the state to produce a "product" (a set of services) for the state. The legal agents responsible for the production of this product were the board of directors, who signed the legal agreement between the agency and Outreach. This contract was legally enforceable. As we will see, the requirements accompanying this agreement served to reorganize the work process of the agency. The transformation of the agency took place at the point when the contract was drawn up.

When we examine the objective of the employment agency, as stated in the 1980-81 funding proposal, and the contract between Outreach and the agency, we see that the services provided to immigrant women now had to be measured in quantitative terms. The objective as stated in the original funding proposal was as follows:

> To serve immigrant women, and especially immigrant women of Chinese, Italian, West Indian and Spanish speaking origins, with their employment-related needs. This has been accomplished through individual counselling.

The wording of the contract had been altered slightly to read:

> To improve, *in measurable terms,* the employment and employability of immigrant women who have experienced difficulty entering the labour market. Special emphasis will be given to employment services for individuals and groups of women of Chinese, Italian, West Indian and Spanish speaking origins. (My emphasis)

Similarly, proposed activities of the employment agency were specified in enforceable and measurable terms in the contract between it and Outreach.[2]

Analyses of the different documents show that while the activities in the funding proposal dealt almost exclusively with services to clients, the contract included additional activities such as "client marketing" and placement of clients in employment *and* training programs.[2] Provision of services now included those to clients *and* to employers. As well, the contract stipulated the relationship between EIC and the agency. A close reading of the contract thus reveals the mandate of the Outreach Program in relation to the overall mandate of EIC: the regulation of the labour force through the voluntary sector. The "product" purchased by Outreach from the agency had to do with (a) the articulation of immigrant women to employers who made use of this specific labour pool, and (b) the referral of immigrant women to training and other programs provided by the state. The contract was the legal means of insuring that this product would be delivered by the employment agency.

How did Outreach ensure, at the daily level, that the employment agency was indeed producing this "product"? For analytical purposes, I have divided the accountability structure, which tied the activities of the employment agency to the coordinated functions of the state, into two components: a hierarchical reporting system, and textual accountability. They are described separately below. In reality, however, the reader should bear in mind that they were part and parcel of the same organizational structure.

## A Hierarchical Reporting System

The fundamental requirement of the funding protocol was the integration of the employment agency into a system of accountability internal to EIC. A close working relationship between members of the agency, especially the coordinator (representing the staff), and the personnel at the different levels and departments of EIC, was not only essential but mandatory. Diagram 1 provides a schematic representation of the reporting system tying the employment agency to EIC. It summarizes the respective responsibilities of the actors involved at each level in relation to a time frame. Here is how it works:

The agency, through the coordinator and the board[3], was obligated to report to a local CEC (Canada Employment Centre) designated by Outreach, located within the same administrative district as the agency, and the regional office of the Outreach Program. The various reports (see next section) required by Outreach, were prepared and submitted to the local CEC by the coordinator on a regular basis.

Within the local CEC, a project officer was assigned to oversee the submission of these reports and ensure that the information was submit-

DIAGRAM 1

## The Reporting System

| Location of Individual | Rank and Position of Individual | Tasks and Responsibilities of Individual | Appropriate Time Frame[2] |
|---|---|---|---|
| Employment and Immigration Regional Office[1] | Outreach Consultant | -oversees agency's overall performance<br>-checks and approves reports from agency<br>-assesses and approves funding proposal(s) of agency<br>-issues cheques to agency for monthly expenditures | 4th week of month |
| Local CEC Office[1] | CEC Manager | -checks reports from agency<br>-approves reports<br>-forwards reports to Regional Office | 3rd week of month |
| Local CEC office[1] | CEC Project Officer | -receives reports from Coordinator<br>-checks reports and supervises bookkeeping of agency<br>-oversees agency's operation<br>-ensures cooperation between agency and other CEC programs | 2nd week of month |
| Employment Agency | Coordinator | -gets various records from staff<br>-compiles various reports<br>-submits reports to CEC Project Officer<br>-coordinates agency's operation | 1st week of month |
| Employment Agency | Employment Counsellors | -record Attendancy Sheet and Service Sheet<br>-make summary of clients' records in Clients' Record Book | |

[1] Extra information on aspects of the agency's operation can be requested at any time by any of these levels

[2] This is the schedule for the compilation of the Monthly Financial Report (MFR) and the issuance of the following month's expenditure cheque by Outreach.

↑ —reports to

ted in a proper format. His mandate was to supervise the bookkeeping of the agency and to ensure and facilitate cooperation between the agency and relevant CEC programs. For instance, when a client of the agency was denied admission to a CEC program (such as ESL—English as a Second Language), the staff of the agency could contact the project officer and he was obliged to look into the matter and, if possible, resolve the problem.[4]

A good working relationship with the CEC project officer, therefore, was essential not only in terms of the funding arrangement but also in terms of the extent to which the counsellors could negotiate, on behalf of their clients, for admission to CEC training and language programs. Furthermore, a congenial working relationship with the project officer could cut down on many potential hassles which might arise from the funding process. The following example indicates the importance of this relationship and the dependency of the agency upon the good will and skills of the project officer, to smooth the way for the agency within the EIC bureaucracy.

> The coordinator rounds up two of the counsellors in the board/staff room. Apparently, the agency has to demonstrate good relationship with CECs. In the Quarterly Statistical Report, the Outreach consultant notices a drop in the agency's utilization of Manpower (EIC) programs. ... This seems to be a major problem which must be well handled. One counsellor exclaims that it seems that the new CEC project officer is not doing an adequate job for the agency. The previous project officer used to work up, in his report, his involvement with the agency to show that indeed the agency maintains good contact with Manpower. It seems that the new project officer hasn't been doing that and so it appears to the Outreach consultant, his superior, that the agency hasn't been doing a proper job of maintaining a good relationship with Manpower.
>
> (Fieldnotes, September 16, 1981)

Once the CEC project officer received the appropriate reports from the employment agency, most notably the Monthly Financial Report (MFR), he went through them to see whether the information submitted was acceptable. If they were, he presented these materials to the CEC manager for approval. The CEC manager had little direct interaction with the employment agency. Usually his approval of the reports was a matter of routine. However, delay in approval was part of the process because he was in charge of all the business arising from his office. Frequently it took him at least a week to get the MFR approved. Once he approved the reports and thereby the agency's budget for the following month, he sent this information on to the regional office of Outreach for final approval.

Within the Outreach regional office, a special consultant was assigned to oversee the agency's affairs. The assignment of Outreach projects to the consultants was done according to geographic and/or electoral districts. There were nine districts in the Ontario region, and three consultants for the entire region. This meant that the workload of each of the consultants was heavy, and further delay was built into the processing of funding for projects.[5] The mandate of the Outreach consultant was to approve the budget of the agency and monitor its overall performance. Further questions about the operation of the agency could be raised at any of these levels. From time to time, information additional to the standard reports was indeed requested, and the agency had to respond promptly before its monthly expenditure was approved.

One example concerning this kind of request occurred shortly after I began fieldwork at the agency. After the submission of the MFR, the coordinator received a phone call from the Outreach consultant requesting information on the clients' ethnic backgrounds. Although the agency could produce these statistics based on the information entered into the Clients' Record Book (CRB, see next section), they were not readily available. To compile this information, the coordinator had to go through the entire CRB and pull out the relevant parts of the record, a tedious and time consuming task that took time away from the coordinator's routine administrative work and from counselling.

Another example of this additional demand was that the Outreach consultant would ask for a breakdown of the total number of "employer contacts" made in relation to job categories (e.g. factory, restaurant, retail) for a certain time period. Owing to increasing client in-take and administrative tasks, the agency was frequently behind in its record keeping. Thus, not only was this kind of information not readily available because the agency did not keep these statistics, such a request necessitated the immediate updating of certain kinds of records at a moment's notice. In this case, the coordinator had to ask the other counsellors to stop their respective work and compile the information on an individual basis, which was then given to her for final tabulation. At times, in order to respond to the demands made by the funding program, the agency had no choice but to close its doors to clients for an afternoon or for a day. When this occurred, its overall record on client in-take and job placement would in turn be affected. Furthermore, when this kind of unexpected demand arose and took the counsellors away from their regular routine, they felt resentful; the antagonism was frequently directed at the coordinator who was the person directly making the demand. This was one way in which tension was generated in the daily operation of the employment agency.

The coordinator did, especially in the initial period, attempt to resist additional demands by Outreach. The following incident, recorded during an early period of the fieldowrk, serves to shed some light on the effort exerted on the part of the agency to circumvent the progressive interference of the funding body with its routine:

> I made some suggestions as to how the coordinator could improve the record keeping system, and I treaded on a very sensitive area! The most serious problem of the agency, as she sees it, is the enormous amount of statistics the staff has to keep. She kept emphasizing, during our conversation, that there was *no way* that they could possibly do any more. It finally struck me that she was afraid I would go in there and start changing things around to give them more work. So I reassured her that I would, under no circumstances, ask them to do extra work just for my research, or for a "better" record keeping system...
>
> I was ... impressed with her ability to hold her ground. She refuses to let the record keeping interfere with the work of the agency, and that's a principle that she holds. She said that when Manpower insisted on getting more and more statistics, she got mad and told them they could come and do it themselves; the staff didn't have that kind of time.
>
> (Fieldnotes, February 19, 1981).[6]

The organization of this reporting system meant that delay in the administration of funds was built into the whole funding process because Outreach would only pay for the services after they were delivered. Aspects of these services, furthermore, were subject to scrutiny at any time if they were deemed to be incompatible with the "product" expected by the funding program. One consequence of the funding process was the continuous feeling of "crisis" one experienced working in a community agency of this sort. When the monthly cheque was delayed, the coordinator had to use her ingenuity to figure out how to pay the rent and other bills, and it could throw the daily routine of the agency into temporary turmoil. When there was a major delay in the approval and allocation of the annual grant, such as when the 1981-82 budget was renewed only on a short-term basis, the agency could plunge into a deep financial crisis.

This kind of funding arrangement also necessitated a different division of labour among members of the agency. Outreach generally did not provide complete funding requested by the agency. Additional funds to cover the operation of the agency had to be raised continually in any fiscal year. With increasing volume of case work and administrative responsibilities, the staff could not undertake fund raising in addition to their daily work. This responsibility was relegated to board members, who then became progressively involved in the running of the agency. This involvement finally culminated in conflicts between the board and the staff, which I will discuss in Chapter 5.

## Textual Accountability

The "product," for which funding was granted, was given shape and visibility through an accounting system which involved the production of various documents. This accounting system was stipulated by the contract, and included basic financial information, as well as statistical and other data on clients.

At first glance, the amount of information required by Outreach did not seem excessive. Only three kinds of documents were to be submitted on a regular basis: the Monthly Financial Report (MFR), the Quarterly Statistical Report (QSR), and the Semi-annual Narrative Report (SNR). The bulk of the record-keeping appeared to be internal to the employment agency, and was not required by the funding program. However, careful examination reveals that these two seemingly separate documentary processes were in fact part of the same phenomenon, namely, the requirement by Outreach (and to a lesser extent other funding bodies) for the agency to conduct its activities in a certain manner. There are two aspects of the documentary process: first, the proper management of funds allocated by Outreach. This was controlled primarily through the Monthly Financial Report (MFR). Second, the production of the agency's services as a "product" for which funding was provided. These services were defined and made accountable through two major documents: the Quarterly Statistical Report (QSR), and the Semi-annual Narrative Report (SNR).

In order to produce the information for the three reports required by Outreach, an elaborate accounting system had to be devised. This requirement introduced a new work process into the employment agency. Diagram 2 summarizes the various documents and forms used by the employment agency to generate the information required by Outreach. I will not describe the processes involved in producing these records in detail. Much of this description would be technical and would distract the reader from the points I wish to elucidate. I will use one example here, the production of the Quarterly Statistical Report (QSR), to illustrate the amount of work involved in ensuring the proper production of these documents. As already discussed in Chapter 1, textual coordination is an essential constituent of ruling in our society. In terms of the employment agency, the various reports served to ensure that the

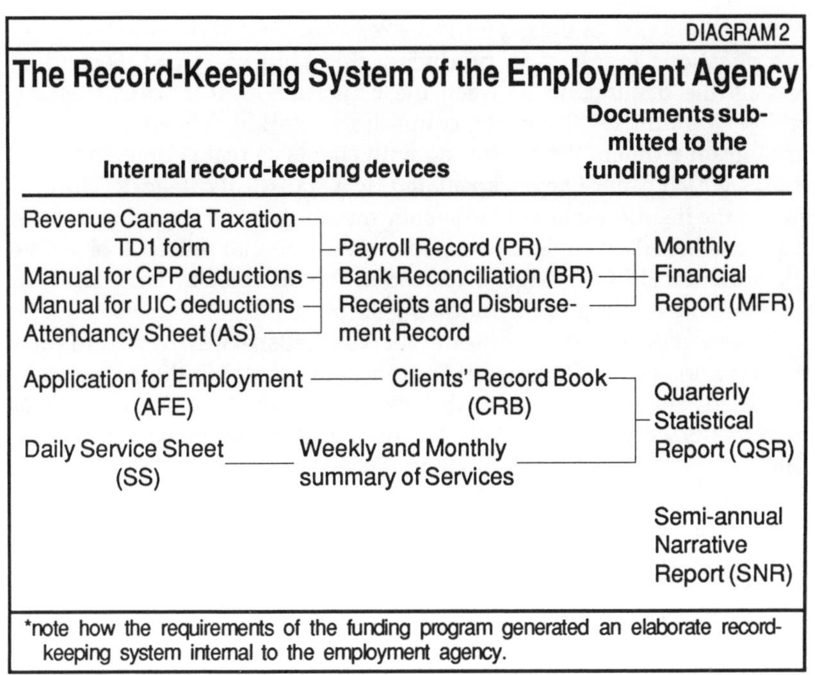


*note how the requirements of the funding program generated an elaborate record-keeping system internal to the employment agency.

product produced was indeed what the funding program was interested in buying.

One of the central concerns of state funding for community groups was that funds be administered in accordance with the guidelines of and agreement with the particular funding program, so that there would be no misuse for purposes other than those agreed upon. To maximize efficiency and uniformity within EIC, standardized bookkeeping procedures had been developed and were required to be followed by all funding programs and their projects. All projects funded by EIC, therefore, essentially followed the same set of bookkeeping procedures and filled out the same set of forms. While this was true, the complexity of the bookkeeping system of individual projects depended on two things: (a) the nature of the particular funding program (which determined the amount of information required); and (b) the complexity and structure of the projects themselves. Thus, when the employment agency was funded under the Canada Works Program as an experimental project, the bookkeeping procedures were simpler than at the present time, due both to the specific requirements of the Outreach Program and the expanded functions of the agency itself.

To produce the information required by the QSR, for example, the coordinator had developed a set of internal procedures for the agency to handle this requirement (see Diagram 2). I want to give a brief account of the production of the QSR for three reasons. First, it demonstrates the complications involved in producing this kind of record. Second, it reveals the disjunction between the construction of a "documentary reality" (Smith, 1974) and the counsellors' working understanding of immigrant women. When dealing with clients as real people, there are things which cannot be encapsulated by a statistical category. Third, it shows the insidious shift in the agency members' view (board and staff), from one based on subjective experience, to one that relied on objective (documentary) knowledge. The reader should refer to Diagram 2 to facilitate the reading of the following account.

To ease the calculation of the number of clients served in order to enter it into various sub-categories of "numbers of clients" in the QSR, services provided, and other items in the QSR, at least three sets of additional documents were involved. When a client visited the agency for the first time, she was required to fill out an Application for Employment (AFE) form in English. This form contained basic information on the client, such as her name, address and phone number, date of birth, marital status, social insurance number, country of origin, type(s) of job(s) sought, as well as more detailed information such as educational background, level of English proficiency, previous work experiences, etc. This was the basic information which every counsellor had on her clients. On the back of the form was space for the counsellor to write down services provided for this particular client, and other relevant information to enable her to make an appropriate placement (see Chapter 4).

The counsellor's comments on the clients were confidential, but selected information on each client (name, social insurance number, telephone number, age, marital status, referral source, years in school—education, country of origin, language spoken, and dates and types of services provided) was entered into a Client's Record Book (CRB), which constituted the agency's overall record on its clients. The CRB was used by the coordinator to calculate the statistical data requested by Outreach for the QSR. A number was assigned to each client, so that the user of the CRB could tell, at a glance, the number of clients served by the agency on a monthly and cumulative basis. The CRB was arranged according to Outreach's fiscal year to facilitate the calculation of statistics.

In addition to the AFE form and the CRB, the counsellors were required to fill out a daily Service Sheet (SS), so that the coordinator could tabulate the kinds and numbers of services rendered on a weekly and monthly basis. Although the SS was supposedly developed for internal purposes, the categories used were based on those requested by Outreach for the QSR. An interesting and important point concerning the SS is that while the counsellors were requested to fill it out daily, not all of them, in fact, had the time to do so. They usually filled it out impressionistically at the end of a week, when it came time to submit the SS to the coordinator. And it was her responsibility to ensure that services provided by the agency, clients served, and the number of jobs available arrived at a reasonable balance so that questions about the reliability of the data would not be raised by the funding body.[7]

It should be noted that the above was not a clearly defined division of labour, but rather something which evolved out of the development of the agency. While the counselling process had a clear focus, since it was what the agency was set up to do, the administrative work was much more *ad hoc* and less well defined. In fact, when the coordinator quit the summer I was doing fieldwork there, there was no job description for her position. The coordinator's position *vis-a-vis* that of other counsellors was thus a problematic one.

In order to make the compilation of the QSR easier, the coordinator summarized some of the items asked for in the QSR, such as the number of clients served, supportive counselling provided, placements made, and various referrals at the end of each month. As she informed me on one occasion when I questioned her about the compilation of various kinds of statistics, if she did not get into the habit of tabulating information according to the categories and format required by Outreach on a regular basis, it would be practically impossible to do it every four months; with all the details to coordinate around the agency, she simply could not remember all the procedures if they were not routinized.

Together with this increasingly complex and elaborate record keeping system was the setting up of a comparable filing system for easy retrieval of the various kinds of information recorded. This, again, was the responsibility of the coordinator. From this example, we see clearly how funding requirements penetrated and reorganized the internal work process (notably the coordinator's job) of the employment agency. There was a gradual shift of the coordinator's work from counselling to management and administration. The development and coordination of the record keeping system became a specialized task in and of itself.

It should be understood that strictly speaking, the development of internal record keeping systems was not imposed upon the agency by Outreach. As the agency itself grew, there was a perceived need, by counsellors, to keep track of their clients, because they could no longer remember all their clients and the kinds of services provided for each of the clients. Meanwhile, board members, who were not involved in the daily operation of the agency, also felt a need for detailed and proper record keeping. This was one way they felt they could learn about the operation of the agency. In this way, members' knowledge of the agency was rendered more and more "objective" and detached from an experiential base.

As I stated in Chapter 1, documentary-based information systems are a means through which ruling is accomplished in modern societies. Recent studies (eg. Campbell 1984; Campbell and Ng, 1986; Muller, 1987) have shown that the reliance of documentary-based information systems is problematic for front-line workers who confront people's lives as a totality, and not simply as discrete categories. As Smith (1974) demonstrated, the "documentary reality" references the organizational (in this case funding) requirements, as we saw in the tabulation of the Service Sheet (SS); it doesn't represent what actually happens.

One problem of the QSR expressed by the coordinator and other counsellors was that the categories provided in the QSR did not give an adequate picture of (a) the amount of work carried out by the agency and (b) the reality of immigrant women in the job market. Indeed, the coordinator experienced persistent difficulties in working up and organizing the work process of the agency to conform to the categories provided by, and terms of reference meaningful to, Outreach. One incident in particular, brought this kind of disjunction between the documentary reality and what actually happened into focus.

The incident concerned a query, by Outreach, of two categories, "new clients" and "re-registered clients" in one of the agency's QSRS. This occurred shortly after the coordinator left the agency and before a new coordinator was appointed. The agency was contacted by Outreach about an ambiguity which the Outreach consultant detected in the most recent QSR submitted by the agency. The staff called a meeting to discuss the matter, together with other issues concerning the running of the agency, and I was invited to sit in at the meeting.

> The item of interest during the meeting concerns the calculation of clients for the QSR. The category of "re-registered clients" is very dubious. According to the agency's old policy, all clients who have come to the agency for three months are re-registered. Manpower considers a client as a new case after two years. Obviously the agency, with its yearly funding, cannot do that. So new policies have to be devised. We go around that one for the longest time. Finally, it is decided that every client is a "new" client after 6 months. They are considered "re-registered" after 3 months. (Note: These are categories on the QSR forms). One counsellor feels that the coordinator has been doing it all "wrong"... I suggest that the way the category is provided, there is so much ambiguity that it doesn't seem to matter one way or another...
>
> My analysis is that it is not a matter of the lack of a policy. It is that those categories don't tell you very much about how to conduct things in the real world ... but try to convince this counsel-

> lor, who believes that with "proper" administration, everything would be OK.
>
> (Fieldnotes, October 7, 1981)

Paradoxically, this view on the usefulness of statistics, and the "proper" management of documentary information was shared by most members of the agency, even though at one level they knew that the categories given by Outreach and developed by themselves did not fully capture what they knew about the agency's operation or the situation of immigrant women in the labour force. Here is another example which illustrates the gradual convergence of the agency members' view and the requirement of the state.

> The striking thing was around the area of statistical information. The president of the board really trusted stats info. Throughout the interview, she emphasized that keeping stats was a good thing not only for Outreach. It provides the agency with a sense of where it is at—"keeping in touch with the need" was the way she put it.
>
> (Interview notes, the president of the board, November 4, 1981.)

As the above examples reveal, the way in which the ruling process penetrated the internal operation of the agency was not merely through a direct imposition of directives on its mode of operation. More profoundly, as the employment agency expanded and its functions grew in complexity, a set of new accounting procedures (of clients, of employers, of services provided, etc.) also became the internal requirement of the agency itself. The notion of what counted as proper accounting was one shared by Outreach and members of the agency. In the course of its development, the perspective of the agency shifted from one which attended to the lived experiences of the clients to the perspective of an impersonal institutional order. This is a crucial way in which the agency became an extension of the state: not only through the funding requirement which imposed certain changes on the agency's operation, but also through a concomitant transformation of its perspective. Through this transformation, the agency was brought into a collaborative relationship with the state.

Chapter Four

# The Counselling Process

Counselling and placement were the central components of the work of the employment agency. It was for this work that the agency was funded. In the provision of these services, the agency concentrated on assisting women who could not make use of similar services provided by Canada Employment Centres (CECs) and other channels within the formal service delivery system due to language and cultural barriers (Funding Proposal, 1981-82). The first three objectives of the agency, as set down in the by-law provided the overall framework of and direction for the agency's operation.[1]

The role of counsellors, from their point of view, was to act as an "advocate" for the client who, as a result of the "barriers" mentioned above, could not negotiate the activities surrounding successful employment on her own. Thus, while placement of immigrant women was important, educating them to negotiate more effectively in a competitive labour market and helping them overcome various employment-related obstacles, including legal, practical, and social problems was also seen to be an integral part of the counselling process by counsellors. In this way, the agency hoped to improve the status of immigrant women in the long run.[2]

An analysis of the counselling process, however, reveals the double character of the agency's work with immigrant women. It is in this process that the class character of the agency comes into focus. While the intention of the agency was to assist women in overcoming the structural barriers of the labour market and promote their overall status, when we review the counselling process, we begin to see that part of the counselling process involved the counsellor's discretion and ability to work up the client's work experience and skills into "credentials" which could then be matched with the requirements of certain job openings. The counsellor selected, out of all the informatiom given to her by the client, the relevant features of the client's social history and worked them up to conform to the kinds of "skills" and requirements which employers specified in the job orders. While this part of the counselling process was a positive step in helping women with few "marketable" skills to secure employment, it was at the same time the way in which immigrant women were organized into certain locations in the Canadian labour market. The counselling process, leading to job placement, was one way that immigrant women were organized into their class locations in Canada. Thus, while employment counsellors were instrumental in securing jobs for women in a competitive job market, it also came to operate on behalf of the state apparatus for the organization of one segment of the labour force. The work of the employment counsellors constituted a determinant component in facilitating labour market processes by producing immigrant women as a distinctive kind of labour with certain skills and qualifications—as "commodities," and in organizing the relation between immigrant women and their potential employers—the buyers of this distinctive kind of labour.

As we will see in the following account, gender and ethnicity (defined primarily in terms of language in this case), were important ingredients in the screening process of clients. On the other side of the counselling process was the requirement, by some employers, of women belonging to certain linguistic and ethnic groups. In the in-take procedure and interview session, we see the way in which gender and ethnicity entered into the organization of immigrant women's class locations in Canada.

The production of immigrant women as "commodities" was accomplished through documents. In the counselling process, we will see how women's work histories were recorded to conform to the types of jobs and requirements requested by employers. The documentary process mediated the accomplishments of immigrant women as a particular kind of labour in the labour market, and enabled the matching of clients to available job openings. In turn, the records on clients, notably the "Application for Employment" (AFE) form, formed the basis for calculating the statistical information requested by Outreach, thereby providing for the agency's articulation to the state apparatus.

The following account of the counselling process is aimed at displaying the organizational (state and labour market) relations involved in counsellors' work. As such, it is not just a description of a "typical" counselling session. The point to note is that although there were different "styles" of conducting interviews with clients (for instance, some counsellors wanted to remain fairly formal whereas others might adopt a more casual attitude), the counsellors had to satisfy certain requirements basic to the agency and to the "successful" placement of clients in available jobs. Her view on what a successful placement might be was shaped by the employer's satisfaction and the statistical requirements of Outreach.

## The In-take Procedure

The in-take procedure was the first moment of the screening process which took place at the employment agency. The receptionist ensured that the clients were female (men were referred to other agencies) and were eligible for services according to the agency's mandate. At the in-take, women were asked to fill out an AFE form (see Diagram 3) in English, and were further screened in terms of their racial/ethnic backgrounds and linguistic abilities. They were then matched to a counsellor according to these criteria. If a client spoke English fluently, her racial or ethnic origin became less important in this matching process because any counsellor would be able to communicate with her.

As the caseload of the agency increased, women other than the ethnic and linguistic groups which the agency was funded to serve were refused service. Unless they could speak English and a counsellor was willing to undertake the case, they would be referred to other community agencies. The in-take thus screened out individuals who were deemed ineligible for the agency's services by virtue of their ethnic backgrounds. Once the AFE form was filled out, a client could proceed to see a counsellor, and the interview process began.

## The Interview

As a matter of fact, very few clients could fill out all the items on the AFE form easily. Even when a client knew English reasonably well, inevitably she would fill in information which was irrelevant to what the counsellor wanted to find out. In the ensuing interview with the client, in addition to finding out the client's marketable skills and the kinds of jobs she wanted, it was also crucial for the counsellor to find out information on the client relevant to the agency's organizational requirements, which

DIAGRAM 3

## Application for Employment*

(1) Date: ____________
(2) Type of job sought: ____________

(3) Name: ____________ (4) Tel: ____________
family first middle

(5) Address: ____________

(6) Date of birth: ____________ (7) Social Insurance No.: ____________

(8) Years in Canada: ____________ (9) Country of origin: ____________

(10) Marital status: ____________ (11) No. of children: ____________

(12) First language: ____________

(13) Immigrant status: ____________

| (14) English: | Yes | No | Little |
|---|---|---|---|
| (14a) Speak | | | |
| (14b) Read | | | |
| (14c) Write | | | |

(15) Education record:

| School | grade completed | date completed | course studied | certificate received |
|---|---|---|---|---|
| (15a) Grade | | | | |
| (15b) High | | | | |
| (15c) College | | | | |
| (15d) Technical | | | | |
| (15e) Others | | | | |

(16) Employment record (Most recent employer first)

| (16a) Company | (16b) Where | (16c) Position | (16d) Salary | (16e) When |
|---|---|---|---|---|
| | | | | |
| | | | | |
| | | | | |

(17) Referral Source: ____________

(18) Other Information: ____________

| (19) Date Interviewed | (20) Counsellor | (21) Type of service—remarks |
|---|---|---|
| | | |
| | | |

etc.

(22) Case closed: (22a) when ____________
(22b) why ____________

*This diagram is based on the AFE form of the employment agency. Numbers have been added to the items on the form for easy identification.

included the information necessary for the compilation of the statistics and for a successful placement. The AFE form was used as a way of initiating a dialogue between the counsellor and the client, as well as a way of organizing the interview.

In the interview, the counsellors invariably referred to the application form to begin the process, and used the form as a basis for eliciting information from the client. Filling in the form organized the interaction between a counsellor and her client. For example, if a client began to discuss things which were not central to the categories on the form, the counsellor would redirect the conversation or cut the client off altogether, so that the discussion would return to what the counsellor needed to know to fill in the form properly.

The interview process was central to the agency's work with immigrant women because it was here that the clients of the agency were screened and matched to jobs available in certain sectors of the labour market. It is in this process that the class character of the agency's work becomes more visible. This includes three major features. Firstly, in the interview, the counsellor selected the relevant features of the clients' work histories and translated them into the kinds of "skills" and "experiences" specified by employers, thereby organizing them into available job openings. In the screening process, the counsellor also engaged in a "classifying practice" by selecting out women with differential skills and inserting them into different locations in the occupational hierarchy. Secondly, in the interview, the counsellor through questioning the client worked up her background as "credentials" relevant to the job market. In this way the counsellor helped employers screen potential employees, so that the counsellor herself became an agent for the employers as well as an "advocate" of her clients. The counsellor effectively became a "gatekeeper" (Erickson and Shultz, 1982) of immigrant women's entry into the labour market. Finally, an aspect of the counsellor's work involved socializing clients into the "rules" of the Canadian labour market. This included explicit instructions to clients about attributes desired by an employer (e.g. punctuality, cleanliness, swiftness, and "reliability"), and implicit transformative work on the clients' experiences into the terms and categories used by employers (e.g. translating a vague statement of the kinds of tasks which a client could do to specific skills and work experience). These features were woven into the entire counselling process, and the transformative work took place most notably during the initial interview phase when the counsellor attempted to complete the AFE form with a client.

During the interview, the information elicited from the client was evaluated according to a set of categories on the AFE form. Usually, the interview session began with questions asked by the counsellor of the client's proficiency in English. Did she understand any English? How much? Had she ever taken an English (ESL) program? Where and for how long? (See Item 14 of the AFE form.) A client's proficiency in English was seen to be crucial in placement. Although the jobs available through the agency were directed primarily at the non-English speaking segment of the labour force, the ability to understand basic English was an asset in most cases (see also Janke and Yaron, 1979:8). It opened up more possible areas of employment for the client, as most employers preferred workers who could understand basic instructions, especially when the workers did not have previous work experience in that particular industry or business, and had to go through a period of training.

Educational level (Item 15 of AFE) and previous work experience (Item 16 of AFE) of a client were also chief areas to cover in the interview. Since very few of the clients had more than secondary education, and many only had elementary education, discussion about educational background was a cursive part of the interview. Added to this was that levels of education had little relevance to many employers who placed job orders with the agency, so long as the client could understand instructions and do the work (see Janke and Yaron, 1979:7).

Work experience and skills, on the other hand, were a problematic and lengthy part of the interview process for both the client and the counsellor. While work experience and its concomitant skills were important to establish a client's employability, because of the nature of work commonly available to non-English speaking and working class Black immigrant women (which usually comprised either menial work requiring a host of taken-for-granted skills, such as domestic skills, or highly repetitive and differentiated work), it was usually difficult for them to describe what they did and what the work involved. Many clients did not even remember the name of their last employer or the location of their work place. A typical answer from a client, when asked about her past employment, would be: "Somewhere around Main Street" or "the factory that made plastic things," with the client unable to describe the commodity the factory produced. Regarding her work skills, the client was frequently just as vague: "I did what everyone else did," or "I put screws into these round things, you see." The following example from my fieldnotes, recorded when I was acting as a counsellor at the agency, illustrates some aspects of this process and how a vague description of tasks was worked up into a specific job category by the counsellor.

> I tried to get her to explain to me what she did in the last place she worked. She said, "Everything. Just like all the other people." I told her it didn't tell me what she did and explained to her that she

needed to explain her work to me so that I could tell what jobs would be suitable to her.

It was difficult for her to do that. She tried quite hard to explain: They manufactured plastic basins. Like, the basins/sinks were plastic and they came out of a machine. Then she (and other workers) would put screws into the basins. They would wash them first. She also did some general clean up work, like wiping up the mess and so on.

As I was questioning her, I realized what I was doing was to try to categorize what she did so that (1) I could identify what kind of work she was looking for, and (2) I could explain to the employers what this client's skills were when I phoned them up. But her description was so vague that after going around the subject several times, I still couldn't figure out what this factory did.

(Fieldnotes, July 2, 1981)

In the case of this client, since I was unable to establish her precise skills based on the interview, I put down "general factory work" after "type of job sought" (Item 2 of AFE form) on her AFE. The information entered here was crucial because the type of job sought recorded on the client's record, together with her employment record (Item 16 of AFE form), became the basis for matching her to the job(s) available through the employment agency (See Diagram 4, Item 6 -position opened- and Item 10 -job description/requirements- of the Job Order Record (JOR)). Here we see that a description given by the client was translated, by the counsellor, into a category ("general factory work" for the client in question) which could be matched to the description provided by employers. The category of "type of job sought" was important as it became a way for the counsellor to identify the position suitable for the client later on in the interview, when she had to place the client in a job opening (see next section).

I want to emphasize the central role of the AFE form in organizing the counsellor-client interaction. It was used to organize the information relevant to the organizational requirements of the agency, the end product of which was to make a successful placement. This understanding of what constituted appropriate information was often not shared by the client. For example, the client did not always remember the precise dates of her employment at various places. For her, having paid employment was the single most important consideration. From the counsellor's vantage point, on the other hand, the duration of a client's employment was critical because this was one way in which work experience could be established. During the interview, then, the counsellor might have to translate a statements such as "I worked there since the

DIAGRAM 4

## Job Order Record*

(1) File No.: _______

(2) Date: _______

(3) Name of employer: _______ (4) Phone: _______

(5) Address of employer: _______

(6) Position opened: _______ (7) Number of positions opened: _______

_______

(8) Starting salary: _______ (9) Working hours: _______

(10) Job description/requirements: _______

_______

_______

_______

| (11) Name of Client Sent | (12) Date | (13) Counsellor | (14) Remarks |
|---|---|---|---|
| | | | |
| | | | |
| | | | |
| | | | |

etc.

(15) Date position is filled: _______

*This diagram is based on the JOR form of the employment agency. Numbers have been added to the items on the form for easy identification.

end of the summer to just about a few days ago" to a specific time frame acceptable to employers (e.g. eight months), and enter this into the "when" section of the AFE form (Item 16e). At times, the counsellor might explore with the client how long she might have worked there by asking the client, "Would you say that it's about eight months then?" In this way, the counsellor was implicitly educating the client about the employers' terms of reference. This did not mean, of course, that every client would see the relevance of this kind of transformative work. But it is important for our analysis to recognize this as part of the socialization of clients which took place during the counselling process.

Similarly, an exploration of the kind of work desired by the client was relevant to the matching process, because it was through a combination of her work experience and what she wanted to do that a counsellor arrived at an appropriate category for "type of job sought" on the AFE form. Included in this part of the interview would be a discussion on topics such as: whether the client would consider shift work; the wage level she was aiming at; the distances she could or was willing to travel to work; and the kinds of job openings which were in fact available through the employment agency.

This is another problematic part of the interview. The client, especially if she had had some work experience in Canada, would aim at the highest wage level and best working conditions she could secure. For example, during the time of my fieldwork, the minimum wage was $3.50 per hour. Most clients wanted jobs earning at least $4.50 per hour, a wage level which was unrealistic for the job openings the agency obtained from employers. Most employers who conformed to existing labour standards and paid high wages, usually for skilled work, had fairly well established recruitment networks, such as through labour unions and abroad (see Lepine, 1983). The industries and businesses which routinely made use of the employment agency for recruitment were those which traditionally employed unskilled workers and ethnic minorities, and which were labour intensive. They were either very small firms or larger firms with over 100 employees which had to become increasingly competitive in an international market (see Johnson, 1982). Thus, immigrant women wishing to obtain jobs with wages higher than $4.50 per hour could not be placed in the openings available through the agency. Owing to the articulation of the agency to this sector of the labour market, part of the counselling session involved familiarizing the client with this "reality of the labour market," which was precisely the labour market constraint under which the agency had to operate. The following example from my interview with a clerical worker serves as an illustration of how the dynamic worked:

> I asked her the kind of work she was willing to do, such as shift work, geographic location (e.g. the distance between her home and place of work; accessibility re: public transit, and the like), whether she would answer the phone or act as a receptionist, etc. I also asked if she was willing to consider other kinds of jobs such as a factory position if we couldn't find clerical work.
>
> I explained to her that the agency usually gets information on factory work, cleaning work and hotel and cleaning type work. We

> don't as a rule get clerical positions because most of our clients don't have that kind of qualification.
>
> (Fieldnotes, July 21, 1981)

***

In the agency's attempt to upgrade the overall status of immigrant women in the labour market by getting them into white collar and para-professional work, counsellors were more attentive to women with clerical and professional skills. In practical terms, counsellors spent time teaching these clients how to write resumes; gave them special "tips" for job interviews; and briefed them on job search techniques and how to get better jobs which they didn't discuss routinely with other clients. The following interview with a lab technician illustrates how counsellors might deal with clients seeking professional and semi-professional work:

> The second client was a lab technician both in Vietnam and in Moncton, N.B. She moved to Ontario about two weeks ago when her husband's and her contracts ended. She worked part time at the university there.
>
> I explained to her the kind of work she was looking for was not common at the agency. There wouldn't be anything available. If positions like that came up, the employers usually wouldn't contact us.
>
> I went through the newspaper as a routine, not expecting much. The kind of work available in the trades section of the newspaper is usually mechanical or plumbing type work. So I decided to look up the different government departments in the telephone book. I tried quite a few personnel departments and got "leads" from them to contact others. I came up with an initial list for her to follow, and asked her to use her imagination to do the rest.
>
> I also told her that she should probably update her resume to reflect the kind of work experience she had in Canada. I found the little booklet at the office on "How to write your resume" and showed it to her while I did the telephoning.
>
> Finally, I phoned the university's job placement centre and got some info re: how to look for lab work on campus. Then we figured out a strategy for her to get through the list systematically, and sent her on her way.
>
> This client was quite thankful for the trouble I went into. Her English was also quite good so the entire interview was conducted in English as opposed to Chinese, which made some things, such as how to go about looking for a job and presenting ourself, much easier to explain. Of course, this client also had a diploma which

> meant that she would not be doing factory work. So the routine for looking for a job of this kind would be more familiar to me than factory positions.
>
> (Fieldnotes, July 21, 1981)

The fact that these women systematically received better treatment from counsellors should not be reduced to a crude attribution of "snobbishness" on the part of counsellors. In reality, they found these women easier to talk to; they usually had something in common from their backgrounds or education which they could share. Counsellors felt that they were more "useful" to these women and their effort was reciprocated by appreciation or gratitude (as the above example shows). Although the class locations of these women seeking work were not identical to the counsellors, the fact that they shared some common grounds facilitated their interaction, and made the counsellors want to try their best for these clients. The natural extension of their effort was of course the knowledge, and the gratification based on this knowledge, that they were successful in promoting immigrant women's occupational status in Canada, albeit only a small number of women were in fact "promotable" in this way.

A related issue is the way in which the counsellor's own class location entered into the assessment process. While most of the counsellors had themselves been "immigrant women" at one time, their present circumstances and class locations were very different from non-English speaking immigrant women who had no money and minimal skills appropriate to an advanced industrial labour process. For many of the clients, especially if they were newcomers, their immediate overwhelming task was to survive; other material and social benefits were secondary. But this urgency was not always shared by counsellors who felt, and from their position rightly so, that other considerations were equally important. The case I am quoting below concerns the interaction between a counsellor and a woman who recently moved to the city and was desperately in need of immediate employment. She brought her two-year-old daughter with her to the agency, as no one else was available to look after the child. Mia is the pseudonym of the counsellor.

> Interview with new client.
>
> Helps her fill out application form. Mia asks about the kind of work she wants to do, taking into account the fact that she has young children, whether she has daycare, babysitter, etc. Tells her how to fill out application form: where to put first name, last name, etc.
>
> Gives her info on daycare. Asks about husband's occupation. Her place of origin. English proficiency.

Finds out whether client wishes to study English. Encourages her to study English because of her future, even though it's difficult at first. Gives her info on free English classes in area where client lives, and schedules of classes.

This client had just moved to the city. Asks about her work experience.

11:23 Interrupted by phone call for a board member. Answers another call. I help with phone call because it's hectic.

11:30 Resumes interview. Goes through work experience of client. Sewing—what kind of machine she worked on before, for how long, etc. Asks whether she has been to Manpower Centre. Client wants to take clothes home to sew. Mia asks if she wants to work in a factory because there is a demand now.

Tells her to wait until she places her children in a daycare. Client is anxious to work. She doesn't want to wait. Mia encourages her to seek daycare so that she doesn't have to work so hard.

11.35: Phones another agency re: daycare situation. Referred to another place. Mia asks about the waiting period for subsidy.

11:41 Gives client info on daycare. Tells client not to worry about jobs until daycare is settled.

11:45 Phones another daycare about vacancies.

11:49 Resumes interview with client. Talks about toilet training. Gives client address of daycare centre. Tells client not to worry if she wants sewing job. She can always get jobs sewing. But immediate thing is to get daycare. Counsels about finances and daycare subsidy. Gives info on translation services if she can't read documents. End of interview.

(Fieldnotes, June 25, 1981)

From this example, we see quite clearly the divergent interests between the client and the counsellor as a result of their different social locations. The client needed a job immediately. But the counsellor's perception and assessment of her needs were quite different. It is not that the counsellor was wrong in advising daycare, which was definitely employment related. The issue is that for this client, the urgency of obtaining wage work was absolute, but the counsellor's assessment took precedence, and the client's request for immediate employment was ignored.

## Job Search and Job Placement

I want to turn now to another aspect of the agency's work which, though much less visible, was equally central. This is the job search process and the agency's relations with employers. In order to arrive at a continual supply of job openings for its clients, employment counsellors had to establish contacts with employers who would place orders with the agency when they needed workers. In the two years since its inception, the agency had established an "employer contact" system. While initially contacts were set up through visiting potential employers in the city who were willing to hire immigrant workers, and introducing the work of the agency to them, by the time I conducted fieldwork there most of the employer contacts were carried out by telephone, and revolved around a fairly stable network of employers.

In addition, counsellors scanned the "classified ads" sections of the major newspapers to keep adding employers to the agency's employer file. The process of selection was fairly random. It was to a certain extent determined by the perceived needs and demands of the clients. For example, most of the agency's clients lived within the city boundaries, especially within the downtown area. Most of them did not have their own transport, and therefore would not be able to travel long distances to work; thus, it would be impractical to contact employers outside the city boundaries. The following excerpts from my fieldnotes illustrate some of the dynamics involved in the job search process:

> I began the conversation by telling the person answering the phone where I called from and what the agency did. Then I asked for the personnel department or whoever was in charge of personnel. When I got the right person, I explained myself again and asked him if he had any position open. At first, I didn't specify the kinds of positions I was looking for, simply because I didn't necessarily know what the place produced. Usually they said there was nothing and hung up. Then I got smarter and asked them whether they needed "general help on the floor." They usually still said no, but it gave them some indication of what position I was aiming at. Generally, they were polite. A few were impatient. A few were very kind and started to explain that they didn't have an opening right now and didn't anticipate any, either because of the mail strike (orders didn't come in) or because of a general slowdown. Some explained that they had a permanent staff and didn't as a rule hire people for long stretches of time. My high point was when I talked with a woman who laughed and apologized that they didn't have any opening. "The only opening we have is for a

very competent, top-notch bookkeeper—no training—so that I can walk out of here tomorrow!"

A couple of places said they did have an opening, but it was heavy work only suitable for men. One said, "I don't mean that we have to hire a man, but no lady ever worked here before. It's pretty heavy work." ...

... I looked under "Packaging" in the Yellow Pages and started the next round of telephone calls. Again, nothing. The only position available required someone being able to lift 50 lb. boxes...

(Fieldnotes, July 22, 1981)

***

After this interview, I phoned up more employers from ads in the newspaper. I explained to them who I was and whom I worked for, then mentioned how I learned about the openings, and asked for details of the jobs. They usually get a bit vague as soon as you discuss wages, as was the case when I called up the factory which makes handbags. I asked what the hourly rate would be. The woman said, "But that depends. It depends on their experience. If they are good they can ask for anything!" I replied, "Anything?" Then she backed down and said, "Well, maybe not too much." So I pressed my advantage and asked, "What's your bottom line?" She finally fidgeted around and came up with a minimum of $4.00/hour. I asked further how soon the worker could be expected to have an increase. Again she hesitated but finally came up with an answer. (I think it's three months, which is pretty standard).

(Fieldnotes, July 29, 1981)

This kind of information, together with the company's name, address, etc., would be entered into another set of forms: the Job Order Record (JOR) (see Diagram 4). The top half of the form was for basic information: the name, address, and phone number of the employer, types and number of positions opened (Items 6 and 7), and space for the employer to describe the nature and requirements of the positions (Item 10 of JOR). The bottom half of the JOR was reserved for the counsellors to fill in details regarding the clients referred to this particular employer, and the dates referred. Items 6 (position opened) and 10 (job description/requirements) were crucial categories, because this information was made use of by counsellors to match their clients to available job openings.

While there were several routine procedures used by counsellors to place a client in a job opening, I will just focus on the relation between the

JOR and AFE of a client, because ultimately, regardless of the procedure(s) used, the "match" was conducted using these two sets of forms.

The job order records were filed in a large three-ring binder according to common categories of work received by the agency, such as domestic work, factory work, restaurant work, and so on. "Sewing" became a separate category during my fieldwork there because it was an industry where there was a constant demand for workers by employers. Once the counsellor identified the category of work the client was seeking (Item 2 of AFE), she consulted the JORS under the appropriate heading in the job order file. She went through the available job openings with the client so they could decide which of the job(s) would best suit the client.

If a suitable opening was identified, the counsellor would phone the employer, tell him about the client, and make an appointment for the client to see the employer. Even when an employer regularly made use of the agency to place his order, very rarely would he hire the client outright over the phone; usually he preferred to look the candidate over himself, or have the candidate go through the firm's application procedure, such as filling out an application form in the personnel department of the company. If the counsellor's telephone conversation with the employer was very positive, she could send the client to see the employer right away, and considered this step a placement. But more often the counsellor would ask the client to call back and inform her of the result of the job interview before closing this client's file.

At this stage of the interview process, the counsellor attempted to provide the client with more details about the job. In the case of sewing, for example, she would tell the client the type(s) of machine(s) the client was expected to operate. There might be a discussion on wages and working hours. The counsellor tried to ensure that the client knew as much about the job as possible so that she would not have false expectations. Frequently, this phase of the interview process also included instructions to the client regarding bus routes, the appropriate things to say in the interview with the employer, and the way in which the client should present herself. If a client was to start a job, the counsellor often impressed upon the client the importance of being punctual.

As well, she might act as a messenger for the employer if he had any special instructions for the client, and so forth. What is of interest here is that by placing a client in a job opening with certain characteristics (e.g. certain kinds of skills, personal qualities with a particular ethnic background) required by the employer and by providing instructions to clients about the special requirements of a particular employer, the counsellor in effect *produced* a client as a special commodity having these special characteristics. When this client joined the labour force, she *became* an "immigrant woman" whom we recognize in the everyday world. This is how "immigrant women" emerge as a social category in Canadian society.

The work of employment counsellors did not only dovetail into the stratification already existent in the labour market; it actively organized and reproduced such stratification. In the above discussion, we see how gender and ethnicity are constitutive features in the organization of immigrant women's class locations in Canada.

Meanwhile, the need of the agency to seek out "cooperative" employers for a constant supply of job orders, as well as the objective conditions of the labour market (i.e. only certain sectors of industries and businesses would hire immigrant women as workers) also made advocacy work almost impossible to carry out in practice. In the counselling process, we already saw that a client's employment needs were not so much determined by what *she* wanted as by the employer's requirements and the types of jobs available through the agency. The assessment of the client by the counsellor was circumscribed by whether this client was a suitable worker for a particular employer or type of employer, the perceived needs of the client herself (eg. desired wage, type of work and working conditions) became secondary to the assessment process.

Since a good relationship with employers was crucial to the placement of ongoing job orders by them, their requirements increasingly entered into the way in which a counsellor assessed a client. This can be gleaned by the language used in the 1980-81 annual report of the agency, a good worker was "dependable" and "reliable" from the point of view of employers. She came to work on time, and did not make a fuss or complain easily. A worker who was late for work periodically or who changed jobs easily was seen by both employers and counsellors to be "unreliable." The counsellors came to take on the perspective of the employers from time to time as they developed working relationships with employers. The following is a case in point. This occurred when I was observing the work of a counsellor. On one occasion I volunteered to help with the counselling. This is what she said when she briefed me about the client I was about to interview:

> This client has been to the agency before. In fact, Rose has already pulled out her file in preparation for the interview. Before asking the client to come into the counselling area, she went through the case briefly with me. She said that this client seemed to have some problems. She (the client) had come in several times and each time did not seem to be able to stick to the job. Either she did not show up for the job interview, got laid off, or phoned in sick. However, currently there are jobs available at a cleaning company and if she was willing I could refer her to that company.
>
> (Fieldnotes, July 9, 1981)

In this example, we see that the implicit requirements of employers came to take precedence over the client's experience. The client called in sick perhaps because she *really* was sick. There were a variety of reasons as to why she was laid off, including shortage of work and intolerable working conditions. However, the characteristics of the labour process to which immigrant women are connected, namely seasonal or cyclical production cycles governed by market relations, poor working conditions leading to health hazards, speed-ups in production, and so on, were interpreted by counsellors as the client's personal attributes. In this case, the counsellor had more or less "given up" on this client. While she was reluctant to close her file, she was very selective about the jobs she referred this client to. She would only let the client know of temporary employment where the client's "reliability" as a worker was not a major consideration and where her own competence in selecting "reliable" workers would not be called into question. She would certainly be hesitant in referring the client to an employer with whom she had established a reciprocal working relationship.

Some counsellors, once they had learned the etiquette of the counsellor-employer relations, would screen their clients for certain job openings. That is, instead of giving clients information on jobs available in a certain area of work, the counsellor decided what a particular client was best suited to, and only gave her information specific to that opening. The client was excluded from having a choice in the available job openings. In this instance, the counsellor effectively acted as an agent for employers, as the following example shows:

> ...Betty screens people...She decides whether this particular job would be good for this particular client. If not, she doesn't even mention that the job is available. This is a fairly common procedure to save time. She does the screening and then lets the client know of the jobs *she* thinks would be suitable.
>
> (Fieldnotes, November 4, 1981)

Furthermore, the requirement of the funding program also entered into the assessment process of clients by counsellors. Shortly after I began working at the agency, I asked the coordinator how a job search for clients was conducted. The conversation led to a discussion of when clients were considered to be "unplaceable" by counsellors. Here is what she told me:

> The client is usually given five chances before her file is closed. That is, she will be referred to five places or be given five opportunities to see if she wants to take the job.

In cases where it is "her fault," i.e. if she fails to show up for an interview; if she is too picky about what she wants to do; etc., she is only given three chances.

Note: I presume that this is where the discretion of the counsellor comes into play. What constitutes too "picky," for example? A certain amount of subjectivity must be present in this process, although there is some kind of implicit policy among the staff at the agency.

After the five or three chances, a client is considered unplaceable. In that case, further counselling is carried out to determine whether a client is suitable for the type of work she expresses interest in; whether she is really interested in seeking employment; whether she needs to take ESL classes or job training; etc.

After this is determined, then the counsellor will attempt to refer her to the appropriate services, or close her file for the time being.

The coordinator explains that, as much as they would like to, they cannot spend all their time with one client. (Note: The funding is conditional upon the volume of jobs they placed. Therefore some decision has to be made as to when a client has to be "dropped" or temporarily disattended to.)

(Fieldnotes, February 19, 1981)

This discussion with the coordinator points out two very important considerations in the agency's work with labour. Firstly, in order to establish itself as a reputable organization, both in the eyes of the "public" (i.e. clients and employers) and the state, the counsellors felt that they had to adopt an "objective" stance *vis-a-vis* the clients. Although the counsellors firmly believed in and were committed to advocacy work, they at the same time recognized that "clients could be wrong." This contradiction surfaced, not only in their work with clients, but also in my informal conversations with them. As a community agency receiving state funding, which was in turn generated by tax revenue, they felt that they had to be "fair" to the "public," the tax payers who included both clients and employers. Indeed, "fairness" became a practice in the agency's work. In the annual report of the agency, it was clearly stated that the agency had taken on the role of mediating between employers and clients, rather than acting strictly as an advocacy body for immigrant women.

In entering into a working relation with employers, the agency had progressively organized its work in relation to the requirements of capital, and had over time unwittingly adopted the standpoint of capital. This notion of "fairness" also came into play in handling disputes between employer and employee, as the following example shows:

> The outstanding event in the morning was that one of Linda's clients was injured in an industrial accident at work and broke her finger. As Linda talked to her, she discovered that the client had been paid below minimum wage. She was indignant and phoned up the factory right away and told the bookkeeper that they had violated the Employment Standards Act. She demanded that they reimburse the client the difference between her wage and minimum wage immediately since she would be unable to work for a while. She then talked with the supervisor on the phone and asked him why the client was switched from the sewing machine to a different machine which caused her injury. Some explanation from the supervisor was given and Linda was obviously less outraged after that. She then called another agency and told them this client needed help.
>
> (Fieldnotes, July 7, 1981)

As I was listening in on Linda's conversation with the employer, I noted that her tone of voice changed from being outraged to being conciliatory. When I questioned her later about the result of the client's injury, she told me that "it was OK" because the employer was "reasonable" in transferring the client to a different machine and that the client was careless in handling the new machine. In cases like this, the action which a counsellor could affect was limited. This particular case was resolved by referring the client to the Workmen's Compensation Board and another community agency. Thus, in helping immigrant women with their employment problems by dealing with employers, the agency also entered into a contradictory relationship with labour by taking on the interests of capital to a certain extent.

The second factor which served as a significant limit to the effectiveness of the employment counsellors' work with labour was the general health of the economy, and therefore the availability of jobs in those sectors which employed immigrant women. When the economy was bad and jobs were scarce, counsellors had much less bargaining power with employers, and they might (and did) have to accept job orders which the agency otherwise would reject. The agency usually tried not to accept jobs paying minimum wage. But during the summer of 1981, when I conducted fieldwork there, jobs were so scarce that counsellors were forced to accept job orders for minimum wage jobs, such as general kitchen work, sewing, and dishwashing jobs.

Whereas the agency could easily black-list employers who violated employment standards when there were more job openings, during periods of job scarcity, counsellors were reluctant to offend employers who regularly placed job orders with the agency, even though they might not conform totally to employment standards. I was caught personally in this dilemma when a regular employer called the agency, and the counsellor with whom he routinely placed orders was on holiday.

> Then he went on to tell me that he didn't want too many of one ethnic group. He wanted them in "groups," i.e. five to ten of each ethnic group, because otherwise they wouldn't get along with each other and the odd one out would leave. For instance, if he had five or six Vietnamese workers, he didn't want a black one because no one would talk with her and she would eventually leave. On the other hand, he didn't want 80% Vietnamese, because then there would be problems and they got to be difficult to control. I was rather indignant and told him so. He said he didn't care whether it was discrimination or not; he was looking at the matter totally from an economic point of view, and he knew what would work and what wouldn't.
>
> (Fieldnotes, July 29, 1981)

But despite my indignation, I accepted his order, knowing very well that the agency could not afford not to have those jobs for its clients at that time. I mentioned this incident to another counsellor during an informal conversation, and asked if the agency had a policy on this matter. She replied that all the counsellor could do was to tell the employer that she could only send the worker(s) with the skills he asked for, and could not discriminate against people based on their ethnic origins; she personally would not refuse the job order. From this incident, we see how ethnicity was used to create divisions among workers; it became one of the means of organizing divisions in certain sectors of the labour market.

The prevalence of minimum wage jobs or jobs belonging to a certain sector of business (e.g. kitchen work) also directly affected the counselling process. In this situation, instead of spending time helping a client to look for the type of work she wanted, the counsellor might spend the counselling period persuading the client to take a job at minimum wage or in a different area of work which the counsellor wished to fill.

In addition, counsellors developed strategies to cut down on the number of clients they dealt with at these times, knowing that in many cases job placement would be futile. One way of doing this was to make appointments with clients, and refuse to see them without appointments. Some counsellors used this tactic to cut down on the number of clients they saw for a period of time when the job prospects for clients were dismal, and devoted the other time to job search. This situation created much tension between clients and counsellors. Sometimes a client's persistence in looking for jobs through the agency, as manifested by numerous phone calls to the counsellors after the initial interview, was resented by the counsellor. When pushed really hard, the counsellor might reply, "I told you there aren't any jobs. We'll call you when there is news—don't call again" in frustration. Clients who did not get the hint and persisted were seen as "pushy." Here, we see how the social organization of employment counsellors' work gave rise to the creation of stereotypes of clients by counsellors. In this process, counsellors from time to time lost sight of the original objectives of the agency and could no longer identify with the clients.

Finally, the requirements of the funding program also penetrated the counselling process. Indeed, the high placement rate of the agency during its first year of Outreach funding not only accounted for its high profile within the Outreach program, it also became the agency's own *raison d'etre* of its work with women.[3]

The placement rates became a measure of its own effectiveness and success within the agency. In order to maintain a high level of placement, ways had to be devised to screen the employability of clients in relation to labour market "needs," which in turn fed into the assessment process which I described above. Interestingly, the strategies used by the counsellors to manage their workload, such as requiring that clients make appointments, also had the effect of formalizing a previously rather informal and casual drop-in approach, putting a distance between the counsellor and her clients. Thus, in pressuring the state to provide funding to and services for immigrant women, the agency also had to confront the danger of having its work redefined in accordance with the interests of the dominant classes: by the state and by employers.

From the above account, we see how the interview process served to select and articulate, as well as socialize, immigrant women into a labour process stratified by gender and ethnicity. The counsellor's work in this selecting and matching process, meanwhile, was part of how a segregated labour force was organized and maintained on an ongoing basis. In examining the counselling process of the agency, we glimpse how class rule is accomplished in a liberal democratic state: not merely through coercive mechanisms, but also through its elaborate funding apparatus which penetrates into grassroots organizations and movements. We begin to see how class is *reproduced* as a practical everyday matter: as people look for jobs and as people go about their daily routine of doing their work. Class is not simply a set of categories based on some objective indicators; it is a dynamic process produced and reproduced through human activities on a daily basis.

Chapter Five

# Effects of State and Market Relations

## The Emergence of a Hierarchy

Having examined the funding and counselling processes, we can now turn to a fuller explanation of the effects of state and market relations on the organization of the agency and its work with immigrant women.

As we have seen, the incorporation process introduced a hierarchy into the agency. The volunteers, who formerly worked in an advisory capacity in relation to the paid staff, now became the board of directors: the body legally responsible for the financial health and welfare of the employment agency. Their responsibilities were clearly spelt out in the by-law of the agency:

> The Board of Directors shall have the following responsibilities:
> a) To ensure provision of adequate funds for the operation of the organization;
> b) To appoint a coordinator of services. On consultation and with the agreement of the Board of Directors, the coordinator shall be responsible for the hiring, firing, and supervision of all staff;
> c) To appoint four signing officers, two from the Board and two from the staff, two of whom shall be required to sign all cheques, contracts and leases, and other official documents;

d) To have ultimate financial responsibility for the operation and file all necessary corporate reports;
e) To fill vacancies which occur on the Board and to report attendance to the Committees;
f) To ensure the implementation of policies as determined by the organization;
g) To propose by-laws to be approved by General Membership at a general membership meeting;
h) To call meetings of the general membership at least three times a year;
i) To elect the three executive officers—Chairperson, Secretary, Treasurer;
j) To fix a head office;
k) To form committees such as Membership, Funding, etc. from the Board, with the possible participation of staff members.

(Article V - Board of Directors, item 3,
by-law of the agency)

As well, the coordinator's position formalized in the by-law (item b above), was entrusted with the responsibility of hiring, firing, and supervising other staff members.

At first, this shift was not seen as problematic. Board members worked more or less as before, in an advisory capacity. The running of the agency was left up to the staff. However, as the agency's operation increased in complexity, through increasing volume of client in-take and additional demands placed on the staff by the funding program, it became clear to the staff that they needed extra and consistent help. The board members were the natural body of people to whom the staff turned. Neither group would have foreseen that the beginning of this collaborative relationship also foreshadowed the growing tension between them.

The board first became actively involved in the agency around September, 1980, six months after its operation under the Outreach Program. This involvement was a result of inadequate funding given by Outreach to cover basic operational expenses. At this time, the agency occupied an office loaned to the project by the original sponsoring organization. It was situated on the second floor of the main office of that group, and the space was shared by several projects and other community groups. The staff complained to the board about crowded space, excessive noise level, and increasing workload, and requested that the board take action to remedy the poor working conditions.

The fact that board members were asked to "do their part" was interesting in view of the changing legal structure of the agency. It signalled the changing orientation and expectation of *all* members of the agency in relation to this new hierarchy. A new division of labour was built into the structure, instituted by the incorporation process. And although neither the board nor the staff were conscious of the ramification of this request at the time, the implicit understanding was that funding matters were the responsibility of the board, and provision of services was the responsibility of the staff. When money was insufficient to run the agency, the staff felt that it was the obligation of the board to become concerned and take appropriate action. It was also revealing that the staff complained to the board about their working conditions, and demanded that the board take action. Whether they were conscious of it or not, the staff began to see the board as employers responsible for some aspects of the agency's activities.

Certainly some board members took their newly assigned job very seriously. They began to negotiate with Outreach to amend the 1980-81 contract for a monetary increase sufficient to cover the rental of a new and more spacious office, and took over funding matters almost completely. This was initially a mutually satisfactory arrangement. As a matter of fact, when the end of the first fiscal year drew near and it was time for re-application, the staff automatically turned to the board to initiate funding negotiation with Outreach.

By this time, the intermediary role of the coordinator between the board and other staff members was firmly established. She related information on the agency's work to the board; in turn, board members relied on her to let them know of the problems and welfare of the agency and to communicate policy decisions to the staff. Board members had little direct contact with other staff members.

## Continuing Funding Problems

Toward the end of the agency's first year of operation under Outreach, the staff again felt pressured as caseload continued to increase. On behalf of the staff, the coordinator presented a report to the board recommending an increase in the operating budget for the new fiscal year. On the basis of this report, the board decided to increase the budget to accommodate three new counsellors and a clerical staff, and to bring the present staff's salaries in line with some other Outreach projects. This decision was finalized in a funding proposal to Outreach in February, 1981.

Three rather untimely and unfortuante incidents, which precipitated the increasing tension between the board and the staff, occurred between the submission of the funding proposal to Outreach and the duration of my fieldwork at the agency. The first one concerned the funding situation directly. The agency was in the last month of its first year funding from Outreach. But despite repeated negotiations with Outreach, no word had been received about the possibility of funding for the new fiscal year. There was a general air of nervousness within the agency. This delay was due partially to the delay in the approval of the overall national budget by the House of Commons. However, when word about the new grant finally reached the agency from the Outreach regional office, the news was not at all optimistic. Not only was there no additional funding, the regional Outreach office only offered the agency a four-month interim contract with a budget at the 1980-81 level.

Furthermore, to be eligible for this interim grant, Outreach requested that confidential information on the clients and additional statistics be released. The staff decided that they could not make a decision on this matter due to conflict of interest, and the matter was deferred to the board. The chairperson of the board felt strongly that such information must not be given to the state as this would violate clients confidentiality, and there followed an intense period of negotiation between the chairperson of the board and Outreach officials.

Although eventually the matter was resolved and a four-month contract was signed between the agency and Outreach, this incident created a permanent rift in board-staff relations. While the chairperson of the board reassured the staff that their jobs would be secure regardless of the outcome of the negotiation, there was much speculation among the counsellors about the agency's future. The perpetual threat to the agency's survival was once again driven home to them. They became painfully aware of the fact that the incorporation process to seek so-called permanent funding actually did not increase their job stability. Moreover, they had lost much of their previous autonomy.

By the end of March, 1981, it was clear that no extra funds were forthcoming from Outreach. To demonstrate their commitment to the agency, the board took initiative and responsibility for a fund-raising drive, which was very successful. In just over a month's time, the board raised enough money to hire a Vietnamese counsellor right away, and later a Portuguese counsellor on a part-time basis. Although this effort raised the morale of the agency's members for a while, it was clear that board members were not just volunteers; they had come to play a central role in one of the major functions of the agency. The following excerpt from my interview notes with the chairperson of the board serves to indicate the changed perception and expectation of the board. This passage concerned our discussion on the statistics reflecting the drop in volume of services provided by the agency in the summer of 1981. Since only an interim contract was signed with Outreach, the board continued negotiations with Outreach for an increase in the budget.

She feels that the agency could possibly have obtained the expansion if the stats were down, but she wasn't sure. She feels that it is critical for the decrease to happen at this time, because the board has been pressuring Outreach very hard and going out to raise money on their own to hire extra staff. She feels that the drop couldn't have happened at a worse time.

(Interview notes with chairperson of the board, November 4, 1981)

Although the chairperson of the board was careful not to appear critical of the staff during the interview, it was clear that she was disturbed by the drop in the agency's statistics. She was further upset that she was not informed about this drop until money had been raised and negotiation was underway with Outreach. She felt that, as the official representative of the agency, she was put in an embarrassing situation to have gone to the "public" and impressed upon the community the vital role of the agency in helping women with employment problems when the statistics showed that less women had been using the agency's services. The pivotal issue here is that she felt fully responsible and saw the staff as employees.

## Contestation of Control

The second incident concerned the recruitment of new board members, over which the board and the staff seriously disagreed. Subsequent to the fund-raising drive, those board members active in the campaign became more involved in the running of the agency. Since the campaign took considerable time and energy, some board members felt that more people who would pull their weight in a crisis situation should be recruited to the board. Whereas the present board was instituted by the staff, this time, board members initiated the recruitment in consultation with staff members. This further heightened the staff's feeling of loss of control, and the issue of whose recommendation (board's or staff's) of new members took precedence erupted into a bitter struggle between the two groups.

In this deepening disagreement, the legality of the current board was called into question by the staff. The argument by the staff was that technically the current board was not elected from the membership, since at the time of incorporation there was no membership to speak of. What we see here is that this division was a result of the structural arrangement of the agency introduced by the incorporation process. More importantly, once this structure was in place, the by-law, developed for the incorporation, became a means through which members of the agency argued their respective cases. The rules concretized in documents, now enshrined by legal authority but which meant little to the members in their normal daily work, were evoked to justify or prevent certain courses of action. This is another way that the documentary process came to transform and organize relations within the agency.

The final incident, which led to the ultimate dissolution of the working relationship between the board and the staff, was the resignation of the coordinator toward the end of the summer, 1981. Two issues were involved around this incident. Firstly, after having worked in the agency for almost three years, the coordinator's resignation at this critical juncture was perceived by most members as an act of betrayal. This perception manifested itself in increasing hostility toward the coordinator, which even an outsider such as myself could not help but notice.

> I go to lunch with the coordinator because I want to find out more about how this dynamic works. She reveals to me that she feels condemned since her resignation. Both Louise and Mary have been very hostile, a surprise to her since she has worked so amiably with these people for three years. She feels that the board is also blaming her. She mentions that the chairperson got upset when she was told that the stats have dropped. The chairperson felt that the coordinator should have told her immediately instead of waiting until the evaluator is coming.[1] ...
>
> The coordinator also feels that she has done as much as she can for the agency, and she doesn't want to do any more, especially since Lousie is blaming her for making a fuss about the stats. She feels that her work has not been appreciated.
>
> (Fieldnotes, September 23, 1981)

The other issue concerned control over the appointment of the new coordinator. Some staff members felt that one of the existing counsellors would be a natural candidate for the position. The board maintained, on the other hand, that the board of directors were legally responsible for the appointment, and they wanted to open up the hiring process. The fact that the board chose to exercise their legal power served to deepen existing antagonism and reaffirm the employee status of the staff. Tension between the board and the staff over these incidents escalated in the summer of 1981 to the point where the two groups could no longer work together. Both groups once again turned to the immigrant community to plead their respective cases.[2]

As members became caught up in this conflict, they lost sight of and did not question how the present structural arrangement had shaped and reorganized the distribution of work and power within the agency. Instead of directing their energy to challenging the existing service delivery system and the working conditions of immigrant women, efforts of indiviudal members of the agency were now re-directed toward internal struggles of the kinds I describe here. My analysis points out that, the tensions generated between the two groups had to do with their respective structural locations in the organization. It had little to do with individuals' "personalities." In the above discussion, we begin to see that an individual's perspective and the actions she took according to this perspective were products of a definite social organization.

***

Toward the end of my fieldwork there, a notable incident took place in the agency which deserves attention. With the collapse of the board-staff relationship, some members of the staff began to explore unionization as a way of circumventing further erosion of their control. As the following discussion I had with one of the counsellors indicates, although the unionizing effort was full of ambiguity, most members saw this step as one of the few avenues of recourse open to them.

> To combat all these potential troubles (arising out of the incidents I described above), the latest development is that Sandra took the initiative to contact OPSEU regarding unionizing. According to Lynn the rationale is that if they belong to a union, then there would be proper channels to grieve this kind of problem. The staff obviously sees the board as their enemy ... When Lynn was asked to join the union, job security was put forward as the major reason. She didn't question it becaue she felt that it would be dumb for a small agency to have two union members and two non-union staff, for example. However, afterwards, she found out that the "real" reason for Sandra to push for unionizing is that she and Louise are considering fighting the board — taking legal action re: one counsellor's failure to get the coordinator's position. To protect themselves from being fired by the board for such action, they decided to join a union. Lynn says that they told her about this after they got her to join, and she felt quite cheated by it. Personally, she would be more concerned about the government's decision to stop funding the agency. She would like to know that if that happens, what the union could do to forestall it.
>
> I have mentioned very little about Wanda, one of the part-time counsellors, up to this point. Her knowledge of this kind of event is minimal, because she is not a full-time staff and therefore has not been lobbied in the same way. Personally, she is against joining a union just because she is afraid of unions (I think). Furthermore, I don't think she cares very much one way or another because she

would be leaving at the end of November, when the funding for temporary staff runs out.

(Fieldnotes, October 7, 1981)

What was clear was the recognition by the staff of their employee status *vis-a-vis* the interest the board, their employer. While the process of unionization by the staff further concretized the employer-employee relationship between the board and the staff, it was at the same time an affirmation on both sides that a hierarchical division had indeed occurred within a previously more-or-less egalitarian group, and this division could no longer be ignored. What is crucial to note is that the incorporation process had created a *class* division within the agency. In pressuring the state to provide funding for its work, the agency was caught in a new contradiction, resulting in a structural divison which had unforseen ramifications for its internal organization and the struggles which subsequently developed.

## Changing Mode of Operation

As we saw in Chapter 3, similar to the incorporation process, the funding process had changed the work organization of the employment agency. Administrative tasks now came to be the exclusive responsibility of the coordinator. Her work with immigrant women became a secondary responsibility. More fundamentally, the funding process also altered the internal policy-making mechanism of the employment agency, thereby undermining its goals.

One feature of a community employment agency of this kind was that the process of policy formation was not enshrined in a documented form. It was fairly flexible, and closely tied to the changing situations of the clients. For example, when a counsellor could not resolve difficulties that developed between an immigrant woman and her employer, or if she had queries about the wages offered by an employer, she would raise them for discussion in the weekly staff meetings. The staff meeting, then, was a place where various issues pertaining to the counselling process could be discussed and debated to arrive at a set of guidelines for future cases. What emerged from these discussions was a common understanding among the counsellors of how to handle certain types of situations. As well, the counsellors took this opportunity to provide each other with much needed emotional and practical support for the often trying situations which they confronted in their daily work. This mode of operation enabled the employment agency specifically, and grassroots community groups generally, to be responsive to their constituencies without being bounded by the rigid administrative guidelines and stipulations characteristic of large bureaucratic organizations.

However, this mode of operation broke down as workload increased and during financial crises. With increasing workload, it became more difficult for the staff members to get together at a fixed time. For instance, toward the end of my fieldwork, and especially between the coordinator's resignation and her actual exit from the agency, practically no staff meetings were held. During a financial crisis, the staff meeting was completely taken over by discussion about funding, to the exclusion of any policy discussion.

The effect of this is that counselling practices became individualized and *ad hoc*. That is, advocacy as part of the counselling process came to depend on and reside in the ideological and personal commitment of individual counsellors rather than as a policy and a matter for discussion among the staff.

In terms of the internal relations among the counsellors, the confusion arising out of the lack of discussion on policy matters manifested itself in a variety of ways, from disagreements among the counsellors about a minimum acceptable wage level for a certain category of work, to criticisms by the counsellors of each other's "style" of work. The following is an example.

> The only event of the day is really when, toward the late afternoon Ling starts telling me about Rosie. It begins after she and Rosie have a shouting match with each other. (I didn't know that it was a fight at the time; I assumed that they were talking about cases and employers).
>
> Ling tells me afterwards that apparently Rosie is just giving her shit about referring a client to a job which only pays $3.75/hr. Rosie accuses her of sending a client to an exploitative workplace. Ling is angry; she states that she doesn't normally send someone who has been working at $4/hr. to a lower-paying job. In this case, the woman has no Canadian experience; her parents just passed away leaving her with two young brothers to support; she needs the money right away. She can't afford to wait for a good job to come along.
>
> Then Rosie starts picking on her about sending clients to jobs paying less than $4.50/hr. Ling gets mad and replies that perhaps then the agency shouldn't take job orders paying below that wage, in which case it also means that many clients with no skills who really need work won't have a chance. She asks Rosie to trust her judgement. Rosie then tells her that the previous counsellor ...

> didn't do things like her; she only took clients in the morning and wouldn't receive clients in the afternoon. Ling gets even more furious and tells her to mind her own business.
>
> (Fieldnotes, November 18, 1981)

Under the precarious funding circumstances experienced by the agency, community work itself became a precarious enterprise for counsellors as wage earners. They could not count on the agency for secure employment. This was very clear from the frequent staff change-overs, particularly during funding crises, when counsellors quit in search of more permanent and better jobs. Thus, the recruitment of staff with appropriate experience, committed to working with immigrant women became a time consuming and difficult task. Since counsellors usually quit on short notice, hiring had to be done quickly. If the agency spent too long a time on the hiring process, the unspent salary might have to revert to Outreach, or the agency might face the possibility of losing the position altogether. Under these circumstances, "cultural" criteria (i.e. ethnic background and language proficiency) became the deciding factors in selecting an incumbent, rather than the incumbent's commitment to grassroots community work and her political orientation. Constraints around the hiring process and the relatively low salary, precluded careful selection of the available candidates, and occasionally the agency might end up with a counsellor whose viewpoint was incompatible with the objectives of the agency. The counselling and placement work became merely a job to be executed, rather than a means of fighting for the rights of immigrant women in the work place.

Although it is true that those counsellors who did not share the goals of the agency would move on quickly to other prospects, and the position would once again be open to other applicants, every time a staff member left, the work of the agency was thrown into temporary disarray. The extra workload of the agency had to be absorbed by the remaining counsellors, who were already under a great deal of pressure with existing workload. Clients might have to be turned away when the workload became intolerable, which in turn would affect the overall placement rate, a crucial consideration of the funding process. The most notable of this kind of disruption to the agency's work process occurred when the coordinator left. Her departure not only created much confusion and added pressure to an already unstable situation; it actually deepened the rift already existing among staff members, as the following example reveals:

> After the staff meeting Nancy, the part-time counsellor and I go to get coffee and tea, as she complains at the meeting that things

> keep on running out and no one seems to be responsible for replenishing supplies. On the way to the supermarket, Nancy tells me that she has also been lobbied around the appointment of the new coordinator and she has told them that she doesn't want to get involved. She also complains about Louise—about her disorganization, etc. Nancy has not been paid on time since the coordinator left, like today, that's why she is hanging around when she is only supposed to work half days. She feels that, given this kind of poor administration, she personally would not favour having Louise as the coordinator.
>
> (Fieldnotes, October 16, 1981)

Thus, every small problem, for an agency this size, could potentially become a crisis if not handled properly. But the proper handling of these kinds of situations required planning and a great deal of thought, which in turn took a large amount of time and energy and which disrupted the normal routine of the agency. The funding process, then, did not only reorganize its work process. In many ways, it dis-organized the work process and seriously undermined its advocacy capacity.

## Organizational Constraints on Counselling

This section will examine some of the the effects of the agency's organizational constraints on the counselling process to see how they affected the agency's work with immigrant women.

The workload of the counsellors was an important consideration in counsellors' willingness and/or effectiveness to help immigrant women with their employment problems. The following figures, calculated for the period between April 1, 1980 and March 31, 1981, give some indication of the caseload of employment counsellors at the agency. The total number of clients registered for services was 1,681; this meant an average of 420 clients per counsellor. The total number of employer contacts made was 5,066, with each counsellor averaging 1,267 contacts with employers in whatever form. In addition, the staff held regular weekly staff meetings (which met more often than the usual once a month due to the funding situation), and attended meetings with other agencies. Indeed, the enormous workload was a major source of discontent within the agency during my fieldwork there, and complaints were made frequently to the board and the funding program. "We have to turn immigrant women away," and "the Centre has found it increasingly difficult to perform its mandate as the ... staffing inadequacies become more and more apparent" were common statements during this period.

The result of this kind of workload was that the counsellors ended up putting in overtime, taking the form of either working through lunch and coffee breaks, or staying late to finish the paper work. An interesting point to note is that the funding program did not make provision for overtime for projects under its jurisdiction. That is, the budget did not allow for overtime pay to workers. Overtime could be compensated for by taking time off, such as a morning or a day, but conscientious counsellors were reluctant to do this. Furthermore, for many, the workload only increased unbearably when they returned to work again, since the agency's budget did not permit the hiring of extra staff to alleviate the work. This, compounded with the unstable funding situation, created a great deal of frustration among the counsellors. Indeed, during the summer I was there, some counsellors began to demand compensation for their overtime by staying away from the office to look for other work, and this situation created further havoc within the agency.

Although the workload of the counsellors was not purely a result of client caseload, in the end, it was their work with clients which suffered. Employer contacts was an area which was taken for granted by counsellors. They recognized that, in order to ensure a constant supply of job openings, efforts had to be made to contact potential employers. This was normally conducted over the telephone. Conversations with employers were relatively brief unless there were complications, and the interaction did not demand as much energy from counsellors. By contrast, counselling work with clients was time and energy consuming, especially when the placement of clients presented difficulties. It is little wonder that at times, the counsellors expressed frustration and resentment of their work with clients, if only because of the length and intensity of contact with clients alone. When counsellors were under pressure, they sought to cut back on their work by avoiding extended counselling sessions or reducing their client caseload. Thus, under time and other constraints, it was the agency's work with labour which was compromised.

In the course of their work, counsellors had developed several strategies for reducing their workload, primarily with immigrant women. These strategies merit some discussion as they shed further light on how the agency's work with immigrant women was shaped by funding and market processes.

As the agency expanded, it became increasingly clear to its members that a further division of labour was necessary. The counsellors' caseload had increased to such an extent that they found it difficult to divide their attention between the in-take process, counselling, dealing with employers, and handling other inquiries about the agency. To a certain extent, the agency was able to find assistance in reception by using students placed at the agency for social work practicum to answer the telephone and conduct in-take, and by having trainees from the provincial Ministry of Labour. However, this kind of help was sporadic. For many trainees, this was their first job; some might be going through retraining after various illnesses (e.g. nervous breakdown). A lot of time was spent by the coordinator especially in coaching and supervising them. Thus, although they did reduce one type of work with which the counsellors had to deal, it certainly was not an ideal situation for the agency.

Another way to manage the uncontrolled visits by clients was to enforce appointment-making. Although this was not a device used by all counsellors, and counsellors did see clients who showed up without appointments, many counsellors increasingly used this technique to keep their caseload under control. Of course, this was not the only reason for requesting clients to make appointments. We have discussed this as a strategy to keep the number of clients down when jobs were scarce and placement became problematic. Appointments were also used to "socialize" clients into the labour process characteristic of advanced capitalism, as we saw in Chapter 4. All in all, this method of managing the workload had the effect of formalizing a previously rather informal casual drop-in approach, and it definitely put a distance between the counsellor and her clients.

An interesting phenomenon concerns the way in which the "mandate" of the agency was evoked to reduce the number of eligible clients when the workload became unmanageable. The by-law of the agency stated that the primary objective of the agency was to "place immigrant women in meaningful employment and to help them with employment related needs;" it did not specify the ethnic groups to be served by the agency. Although no official statement was ever made, the implicit understanding by members of the agency was that the groups served would be changed or expanded to reflect and accommodate the demands of different sectors of the immigrant community. The by-law, as worded, was intended to allow the agency some degree of flexibility in responding to the changing needs of different groups of women.

In the Outreach contract, however, the objective of the agency was reworded and specified for funding purposes: services were to be provided to "individuals and groups of women of Chinese, Italian, West Indian and Spanish speaking origins" (1980-81 contract and 1981 interim contract). Although the 1981-82 proposal to Outreach by the agency stated very strongly that additional counsellors were required to service the growing number of Vietnamese, Portuguese, and East Indian women, this request was not granted. Officially, only services provided to Chinese, Italian, West Indian and Spanish speaking women would be funded.

While in the past, the specification of ethnic and linguistic groups did not present a problem to the agency, with increasing client in-take in the face of the unstable funding situation, the objectives as defined by the funding contract became a method of screening clients' eligibility for services. Women who did not belong to these four groups were discouraged from using the services of the agency; they were referred to other agencies, the reason being that the counsellors could not communicate effectively with these women. In actual fact, some women could speak English reasonably well. But when counsellors' caseloads were heavy, they gave priority to the groups funded by Outreach.[3] This was also true for women on social assistance, work permits, etc. who once came to the agency for help as it was one of the few places in the city to which they could turn. As counsellors were caught up in their own survival, they became more reluctant to bend the rules.

We see here that the "mandate" of the agency, as constituted by the funding stipulation, became a way of organizing the eligibility of clients when the workload of counsellors exceeded the available resources. They began to orient their work toward this stipulation rather than the original objective of the agency, and turned away those deemed to be ineligible for services. In turn, "turning women away" was used as a way to negotiate increased funding from the program.

> The strongest indicator of the Centre's effectiveness in meeting its stated objectives is the great number of immigrant women who make use of its services and its present crisis of having to turn women away because of lack of human and financial resources.
> (Annual Report, 1980-81, p.2)

Finally, scarcity of jobs through the agency led to competitiveness among the counsellors. Ordinarily, when a job order came in, it was filed in the Job Order File under the appropriate category by whoever took the order, so that all counsellors could refer to the file during the counselling sessions. However, when the availability of job openings became scarce, counsellors began to keep their own files on job openings. For instance, instead of filing the order in the agency's job order file, she kept it for her clients. It was only when she could not place her own clients in those job openings that she put an order in the file and informed other counsellors. I noted that one counsellor did that frequently during several weeks in the summer. I was at first surprised when she told me about a job opening which I had not come across in the morning when I started seeing clients, and finally discovered that this was her way of keeping her own pool of job openings. Subsequently, I discovered that other counsellors used this tactic from time to time to maintain their own placement level when there was a drop of overall placements at the agency. Here, we see the way in which a collective effort on behalf of labour became individualized: in order to maintain their own placement rates and protect their own clients, counsellors began to carry out their work in relation to their own gains within the agency, rather than viewing the job search and placement effort as a collective enterprise to be undertaken cooperatively.

In sum, the counselling process was not as straightforward as it first appeared. It was shaped by many considerations, both internal to the agency, and external to it because of its unavoidable connection to labour market relations and with the state. However, these constraints should not be treated merely as external impositions. The requirements of employers, the issue of mandate, etc., became integral constituents of the counselling process which the counsellors carried out as a matter of course. In this way, the counsellor's work became part of the coordinated activities of the state in organizing and mediating labour market demands. This is precisely how class, as a dynamic process, penetrates social life.

Chapter Six

# Class Relations and Community Struggles

## Class Relations and State Processes

This study has been an empirical examination of the internal transformation of the work process and relations of a community employment agency for immigrant women. In the beginning of the book, I asserted that, in order to understand the changes occurring within the agency, we need to revise our theoretical formulation of class. As Gannagé, in her study of women garment workers in Toronto correctly pointed out, orthodox Marxist theory is inadequate to take account of (a) the segmentation of the labour market by gender and ethnicity, and (b) women's dual role in wage and domestic work (Gannagé, 1986:11-20). This is because orthodox Marxists define class primarily as an economic category (for example, Carchedi, 1977; Poulantzas, 1978; Wright, 1976).

Returning to Marx and Engels' original formulation, the present study insists on treating class as a *social* relation which is fundamental to and permeates capitalist productive and reproductive activities. Class refers to the way in which human activities are organized in terms of the productive processes of a particular social formation, for instance, what we have come to identify as labour market processes in capitalist societies (Marx and Engels, 1967, 1970). Thus, class is not simply a theoretical concept which needs to be operationalized (such as by developing a set of socio-economic indicators); it is a relation which is discoverable in the everyday world of experience.

When we take this view of class, we come to see that class relations are embedded in very ordinary features of everyday life: as immigrant women look for work, and as employment counsellors go about the business of doing their work. In the counselling process, class relations, in this case in terms of the organization of immigrant women in certain labour market locations, are reproduced and maintained. Furthermore, we see that gender and race/ethnicity are essential ingredients in the organization of the working class in Canada. Immigrant women's gender and ethnicity are made use of by employers, and consequently by employment counsellors, in organizing the labour force to produce its stratified character. Gender and race/ethnicity are *relations* fundamental to the texture of the organization of productive (class) relations in the Canadian social formation. As such, they are ubiquitous features of everyday life and are accomplished through practical routine activities.

I am not arguing that gender and ethnicity are reducible to class. I am suggesting that analyses of gender and ethnic relations cannot be understood by abstracting them from the particular context within which they arise and come to occupy their unique ontological domains. That is, they cannot be understood without a class analysis in the way in which Marx and Engels expounded it. The phenomenal forms of gender and ethnicity must be located in a particular social formation. When we take this strategy, we see that ethnicity and gender are constitutive features of productive relations. That we can think of ethnicity and gender as separate social phenomena is a product of our kind of society which introduces an artificial separation between economic and social life.

Making use of this expanded notion of class, we saw how class, as a dynamic social relation, was embedded in and permeated the interactions within the employment agency. The incorporation process reorganized the internal relations into a structure of board and staff: employers and employees, with a further differentiation within the staff. In terms of its work with immigrant women, we already saw that employment counselling and placement was a moment in the organization of women into definite class locations in Canadian society. This process produced some women (namely women from Third World countries, women of colour, women with little English or skills suitable for an advanced labour process) as "immigrant women" in the labour market.

The change in the structural locations of individuals within the employment agency was accompanied by changes in their *perspectives*. With the assumption of their legal responsibilities for the welfare of the agency, board members did take on the role, perspective, and responsibility of employers. They came to share the view of the state in the administration of the agency: they became internal representatives of the state. In terms of the staff's relation with immigrant women, there was a gradual transformation and crystallization of the counsellor-client relationship. Not only did counsellors play a determinate part in organizing immigrant women's class locations (which after all was an inevitable part of the function of the employment agency), as time went on they too took on the perspective of employers: of capital, *vis-a-vis* immigrant women workers. It must be emphasized that the shift in the members' perspectives was not a conscious or deliberate move; it was an unplanned process inextricably tied to the transformation of the structural changes of the employment agency, sustained by the funding and labour market relations with Outreach and with employers.

The observation made here raises serious theoretical questions about our conceptualization of "the state." Commonly in Marxist scholarship, the state is seen to be a machine or a set of apparatus which, although not monolithic, nevertheless performs different functions of the dominant classes on behalf of capital (eg. Miliband, 1969; Poulantzas, 1980; Panitch, 1977). According to this view, state funding to community groups is a means of social control (eg. Loney, 1977). The implicit assumption is that the state is somehow over and above us, and that community groups are connected to the state only through the tenuous though important funding relation.

From the experience of the employment agency, it becomes clear that the notion of the state as a set of apparatus, standing above and apart from community groups, is inadequate in understanding how the state works. In this study, we saw how the incorporation and funding requirements penetrated the employment agency's internal organization so that some of its members became part of the administrative processes of the state. As already suggested, the board members were the internal representatives of the state who oversaw the welfare of the agency, while the coordinator took on the responsibility for administering and executing the tasks required for funding and other purposes. *They* were the ones who carried out the activities of ruling.

Following the insights gained from this study and recent re-examination of the state (eg. London-Edinburgh Weekend Return Group, 1980; Morgan, 1981; Corrigan and Sayer, 1985), it is much more appropriate to view the state as the embodiment of struggles between classes (see Cockburn, 1977; Poulantzas, 1978). Thus, the state also fundamentally constitutes a set of social relations which (a) legitimizes certain courses of action, thereby rendering other (alternate) forms of action illegitimate; and (b) organizes how people relate to one another. What is important to grasp is that these social relations are relations of domination and subordination: they are relations of power.

The emergence of a hierarchical division of labour into board and staff indicated how relations within the employment agency were transformed as a result of the incorporation and funding procedures. Furthermore, the agency's ability to work with immigrant women came to depend upon the performance of services and production of documents in certain ways for EIC. Some work, such as advocacy, was no longer central to its mandate by virtue of the way in which the contract between Outreach and the agency was drawn up. What can be seen is that through its funding arrangement, members of the employment agency themselves entered into certain relations with one another and *vis-a-vis* the clients. Thus, it is more useful to think of community struggles as being "in and against the state" (London-Edinburgh Weekend Return Group, 1980), rather than completely outside it.

Central to holding the mandated courses of action of the state in place are documents. From our examination of the work process of the employment agency, we saw how important documents were in coordinating its financial affairs and work organization. Indeed, it can be argued that the agency's activities became the coordinated functions of the state in and through this documentary mode of action: in its by-laws, by a legally-binding contract, and through the generation of various records organized around the budgetary process. These kinds of documentary procedures were not taken seriously by members of the agency. In the words of the coordinator, they just wanted to get them "over with" so that they could get on with the "real" work (ie. working with immigrant women). It was only in negotiation with Outreach for a new contract and when Outreach began to require more and more written information to make funding decisions that some members realized the importance of documents in displaying the agency's performance and providing for a measurement of its accountability and effectiveness. Other members, those involved in direct services, remained resistant to and resentful of the imposition of this documentary organization. Some even suggested manufacturing the statistics, to which the board was violently opposed. This became another area of contention within the employment agency.

In examining the interactive relation between "the state" and community struggles, analysts have paid scant attention to the centrality of documents in mediating this relation. What is revealed in the present analysis is the extent to which the documentation process penetrated and organized the internal relations of the agency, both in sustaining the structural divisions among its members and objectifying (thus transforming) counsellors' relation to their clients. As Smith (1984) and others (eg. Jackson, 1980; G. Smith, forthcoming) maintain, texts are a central aspect of ruling in advanced capitalism: they provide for and sustain the legality of the state. Indeed, texts and documents have become the general mode of ruling in advanced capitalist societies. Thus, it is impossible to understand the relation between state (ruling) processes and community struggles without understanding how documents work in mediating, enforcing, and transforming everyday life. This is an essential part of how community struggles become an extension of ruling in our society. Understanding how textual processes work can thus inform community activities in and against the state.

## Community Struggles and Change

Thus far we have examined and analysed the ways in which the employment agency and employment counsellors gradually took on the perspective of capital because of how the agency was articulated to the state ruling apparatus. This analysis paints a rather grim picture of state funded community services because it doesn't seem to point to any possibility for change. This is certainly the position arrived at by many analysts in the field (eg. Loney, 1977; Morgan, 1981). Community activists, on the other hand, argue that government funding to community organizations was gained through political struggle, and that therefore community work is an agent for social change. Furthermore, given the relative flexibility of community organizations (*vis-a-vis* formal state and other organizations such as the United Way) and the critical locations of community workers, it seems that it is still one of the few areas of work where change is possible. I want to end this book by exploring the possibilities and limits of state-funded community activities as they pertain to the workings of the employment agency, and examine more generally how change may come about through community struggles.

It is important to recognize that the agency's work was not a complete swing to the interest of the government or employers. If it were, counsellors would not experience the dilemmas which frequently confronted them in the course of their work. From time to time, they were effective and successful in their advocacy work. One notable area of advocacy work undertaken by counsellors was to negotiate better wages and better working conditions for immigrant women. It should be remembered that in a "free" labour market where labour, skills and jobs were not regulated and controlled centrally (as in a socialist economy), employers did experience labour shortages as a reality of the production process (see Lepine, 1983).

One characteristic of the industrial sector which employed non-English speaking and Third World immigrant women was the high turnover of workers due to a number of reasons, including poor working conditions, low wages, and the cyclical nature of the industry. Recruitment of "reliable" workers took time and energy on the part of employers. From this point of view, the presence of an employment agency providing free services to employers was an attractive enterprise, because it reduced or eliminated the screening process pertaining to hiring for employers. When the need arose, all the employer had to do was to phone up the agency with a list of specifications, and the matter would be more or less taken care of.

Although in one sense the agency was acting as an agent for capital in this regard, employers' dependency on the "agent" also gave the agency some bargaining power in its dealings with them. Moreover, in this situation employers could rely on the agency to help resolve labour disputes stemming from communication problems. Thus, once the agency was able to demonstrate its usefulness to and establish its credibility with employers, it could drive a hard bargain regarding wages and working conditions on behalf of labour. The following is a case in point:

> The same kind of process also went on when I received a call from an employer I talked with the other day. She was very aggressive and nasty the first time I talked with her about a client who asked for a separation slip. This time, she was much more conciliatory. Apparently I sent someone down there (whom I didn't remember!) and she turned out to be a really "good" worker. Meanwhile, she needed another worker rather urgently and asked me to send another person down as soon as possible. Just before the phone call, I was discussing with Maria how to write the semi-annual report and she told me that both she and Rose negotiated for higher wages consistently when they talked with employers. So I tested out what I had just learned and told the employer that the hourly rate she was offering ($3.50/hr) was simply too low. We have been getting orders with a minimum start of $4.50, and, of course, our better clients would flock to those positions. She immediately raised it to $3.65/hr, explaining that she couldn't pay a new person more than the "girls" who had worked there for a while, otherwise they would scream at her and quit. She then launched into this long story about the difficulties of being a supervisor, how the workers from one ethnic group ganged up on her to demand firing this one worker, etc. The conversation was certainly very instructive to me.
>
> Afterwards, I also felt pretty good about my being able to "learn the ropes" fairly fast. I have certainly become much more aggressive in my dealing with employers, because I found that otherwise

> they really treated you like they were employing you! But if you stood up to them then they backed off a little. Also it put you in a better position to negotiate for better wages. This is a dimension that I hadn't discovered before. I certainly don't remember Susan doing that, but then I discovered from Maria that usually it was Rose who did most of the employer contacts at the agency.
>
> (Fieldnotes, July 29, 1981)

This incident is a good example because it shows that the employer did not always have the upper hand. For this supervisor, her immediate task was to find a "good" worker because of the demand of the market, and she was willing to raise the wage level and make other concessions to ensure smooth production. It also shows how an employment counsellor could put pressure on employers on behalf of immigrant women. Finally, it shows that immigrant workers were not merely passive victims of capital's exploitation. If they were willing to act as a group, they could force the employer to make concessions to ameliorate exploitative working conditions.

As I mentioned in the fieldnotes, negotiating for higher wages was, or could be, an integral part of employer contacts. Meanwhile, the counselling process could be a place where counsellors informed immigrant women about their rights in the work place. Although this may not sound like a very progressive step to most Canadian workers, we should remember that many non-English speaking immigrant women were unaware of their rights as workers, and providing them with this kind of information was a necessary and basic step in advocacy work. The following quote, taken from one agency's reports, illustrates some of the general problems of immigrant women participating in the labour force for the first time. Although the report singled out Asian refugees, the description could be applied to many women who did not speak English.

> One of the most significant developments was the drastic increase of clients from Vietnamese and other Southeast Asian backgrounds. Most of these clients entered Canada as refugees; many have never worked in the paid labour force. Apart from lacking the skills recognized by Canadian employers, they also encountered many problems associated with joining the work force for the first time, including how to identify their own skills and goals, how to approach an employer and negotiate for wages, as well as adjusting to a very different daily schedule. They frequently needed very intensive counselling sessions and follow-up.
>
> (Semi-annual Narrative Report, January to June, 1981, p.2.)

Indeed, most counsellors did this as part of the interview process. This aspect of the agency's work was in marked contrast to the approach of many formal government-operated agencies where clients were left to their own devices after the job referral. It was precisely because of the nature of the employment agency (voluntary and community-based, therefore not bound by rigid bureaucratic guidelines) that gave employment counsellors the flexibility to engage in this work.

Another activity which counsellors took up was to monitor working conditions of the work places in which the agency had placed its clients. Monitoring working conditions was in practice an extremely difficult undertaking, and it was never done to the extent that the agency claimed. Nevertheless, counsellors did take it up and take action on behalf of clients. These cases were documented in the semi-annual narrative reports.

> We also conducted appropriate actions on behalf of clients in cases where they were unfairly dismissed. An example concerns a pregnant woman who was fired without holiday pay when she asked for a transfer to a different department; in this case, we contacted the Dept. of Employment Standards of the provincial Ministry of Labour and filed a grievance with the union on her behalf.
>
> (Semi-annual Narrative Report, January to June, 1981, p.3.)

> On many occasions we have had to go to the Employment Standards Branch with such cases as unpaid vacation pay, refusal to issue separation slips and refusal of official statement of deductions. As well as legislative abuse, we have dealt with discrimination on the part of employers who specify a preference for particular ethnic groups, which has forced us to refuse the employer's job order. We are aware of the law stating the requirement of citizens to report such incidents, but we are not able to verify these cases since discriminating employers have contacted us through the telephone.
>
> (Semi-annual Narrative Report, January to June, 1980, p.2.)

My personal experience negotiating and attempting to monitor working conditions for a fifteen-year-old girl is instructive in this respect, because it sheds light on another dimension of the counselling process. The incident concerned a girl who recently moved to the city with her family from a rural area, and who was desperate for paid work because the family was in bad financial straits. She did not have a social insurance card, and therefore would have difficulty finding regular employment which required official income tax and other deductions. One of the few avenues of employment for this girl was private domestic work, and I came across a woman who urgently needed to have her apartment cleaned. However, I was very worried that the employer would exploit the girl, and therefore bargained very hard with the employer to arrive at an acceptable hourly wage ($5.00/hour) and an itemized list of tasks she could ask the girl to do. I then briefed the girl on her rights, and impressed upon her that she did not have to do anything she did not want to or could not do. I also told her to report to me immediately if she was asked to do more than agreed. Indeed, the whole weekend I thought about her and wondered if things would work out for her.

I used this example to indicate the emotional bond which could and did develop between counsellors and clients. Some counsellors maintained close relationships with their clients and carried out this kind of negotiation on behalf of clients consistently, so that clients would trust them enough to report any irregularities to them. Unfortuntely, this kind of work took energy, and due to the agency's organizational constraints that I described in the last chapter, this activity came to depend on the commitment and orientation (eg. a commitment to labour rights) of individual counsellors, instead of being a consistent policy of the agency.

These steps, though small in themselves, give some indication of the manoeuvreability of community work in relation to a disadvantaged sector of the working population, which has the potential of affecting change, minimally in raising the worker's consciousness of her employment rights. The most serious problem of the practices of the employment agency lay not so much in the absence of advocacy work as in the manner in which advocacy work was carried out. Little effort was made by counsellors to bring together clients experiencing similar difficulties, so that they could gain a collective understanding of the structural conditions of their work and develop strategies to ameliorate these difficulties on a collective, instead of individual, basis. As a group of community workers aptly observed, the ideology of advocacy work focusses our efforts on an individual basis so that advocacy, as it is currently practised, tends to be aimed at resolving individuals' problems (London-Edinburgh Weekend Return Group, 1980). This masks the *social* nature of workers' experiences under capitalism and leaves existing structures unchallenged.

From my conversations with the counsellors, it appeared that counselling was combined with workshops for clients in the earlier phase of the agency's history. However, as caseload increased and as the placement rate came to dominate the counselling process, workshops for clients decreased correspondingly as a priority. This was due partly to the counsellors' lack of time and the fact that the agency was not technically funded to carry out this kind of work.

Toward the end of my fieldwork, one of the counsellors did attempt to conduct a workshop for a group of clients who had problems filling out UIC report cards. She thought that an instructional workshop would eliminate the repetitive task of helping her clients to fill out the cards in counselling sessions. I was involved in preparing and helping her conduct the workshop. Interestingly, after the instructions were given at the workshop and when it was opened to questions and discussion, the clients began to talk about the difficulties they experienced in looking for employment. The conversation gradually shifted from the clients' problems to questions around how the agency obtained its job openings, the structure of the agency, and how clients could participate more actively in the agency. At this point the counsellor concluded the workshop. In our subsequent conversation about it, she expressed the "danger" of giving clients too much information on the agency. While she did not say so explicitly, it was clear that she felt threatened. As she said, "we don't want the clients complaining to the board about our work, do we?"

Another point of interest concerned the other counsellors' reaction to this counsellor's initiative. When she brought her idea up for discussion with the other staff members, it was discouraged. When she decided to go ahead with her plan, she was told by other counsellors that workshops were not part of the agency's mandate and that she should not use office hours this way. (The workshop was conducted on a morning when she normally did employer contacts.) This indicates that counsellors saw their work to be geared toward individual clients rather than groups of clients. From the practices of this employment agency and the experiences of others in community work (eg. London-Edinburgh Weekend Return Group, 1980; Corrigan and Leonard, 1978), it is clear that so long as community work focusses on advocacy on an individual basis and so long as community workers do not recognize how this kind of individualist approach contributes to the reproduction of class relations in a capitalist society, community activities will remain band-aid in character, and will not contribute to fundamental social change. This is not to deny that the potential for change is present, even in state-funded community organizations.

In terms of state-funded community work, another important dimension is the recognition of the crucial role played by documents in shaping and enforcing work relations within a community organization. As we have already discussed, the lack of understanding of the documentary process had led to a drastic and negative transformation of the employment agency's work. Similar to other forms of negotiations (eg. funding), documentary requirements can also be negotiated. This can best be done at the outset of the funding process. Given the legal enforceability of the contract between the groups and the funding program, an activity such as advocacy or workshop can, and perhaps must, be included in the contractual agreement to preserve its centrality in the service delivery mandate of the group. Furthermore, an in-depth grasp of the financial and budgetary processes is essential for groups to discover how to work creatively while relying on state funding. In the Vancouver Women's Health Collective (now defunct), for example, the "paper work" was shared by all collective members; firstly, this took pressure off any one individual to specialize in this work to the exclusion of other work, and secondly all members gained a working knowledge of this aspect of the Collective's work organization (Kleiber and Light, 1978). Other organizations may prefer a different, more specialized arrangement. Anyway, the point is to recognize the importance of textual communication in legitimizing and mandating a community group's work process, especially if the group is funded by the state.

I want to state emphatically, however, that it is impossible to have a formulistic approach to state funding. Funding programs and their requirements vary considerably. Within programs, the way in which they are administered also differs from region to region, sometimes even from one office to another. Some Secretary of State programs, for instance, have less stringent requirements for record-keeping, but lobbying and good personal relations with funding officers (eg. constant verbal reports and visits) may be crucial to the funding process. In other words, the question of how to develop a viable economic survival strategy (while remaining faithful to one's intent and objective) can only be worked out practically in relation to the specific situation of a particular group. It cannot be drawn up as a set of generalized principles and procedures because funding programs are targetted for different purposes and therefore have different requirements.

Up to now, our discussion has primarily focussed on community activities funded by the state. True, state-funded services have become the central locus of grassroots community activities. This phenomenon itself is an indication of how, in its attempt to mediate class struggles, the state apparatus constantly reframes and fragments political conflicts into "social problems" (see Morgan, 1981). As we saw in this story, the impetus of the employment agency in pressuring the state to improve the employment prospects and status of immigrant women was transformed into services for employers and clients through the funding arrangement. Furthermore, energy initially directed at pressuring the state was redirected at resolving problems and conflicts within the agency through the same arrangement. The effort of the counsellors to unionize, toward the end of my fieldwork, is telling in itself.

As I mentioned, the unionizing drive by the counsellors was aimed at protecting themselves from the board of directors. Their action was prompted by their instinctive reaction to protect their immediate livelihood when this was threatened by the funding process. It did not lead to an empathy with their clients who were also workers subject to similar or more severe forms of repressive and exploitative measures in the work place. At no time in this struggle was the hostility channelled directly at the funding program and its personnel. While the rift between the board and the staff was an expression of the struggle between two incompatible modes of organization (ie. egalitarian vs. hierarchical), there was no recognition of the source of this conflict. And while the counsellors sought an alliance with the labour movement as this struggle with the board unfolded, this kind of political alliance did not extend to the counselling process with clients. That is, the counsellors did not see that a cooperative relationship with other forms of working class organizations (eg. labour unions) in the counselling process would be a way of forging a *class alliance* between labour and the advocacy work that the agency attempted to undertake. This is because members of the agency did not fully grasp how their work at different levels (as this analysis has shown) was tied to the ruling apparatus of the state. They saw their work opposing, rather than being a part of, the process of ruling. Thus they did not see that linkages with other forms of organizing, including cooperation with labour organizations, might be a way to short-circuit, or at least ameliorate, the organizational effects imposed by the state through the funding structure.

More seriously, in many forms of grassroots organizing, there has been a tendency to channel the majority of organizing efforts into state-funded services, to the exclusion of seeking alternative forms of resistance. While state funding to community services is an indication of the battles fought and won by grassroots community struggles, we should not forget that community struggles extend beyond the formation of service organizations funded by state programs. There are other terrains of struggles (eg. mass protests, alliances with other movements such as the labour movement) which are equally important and complement the advances made through state-funded community services (see Piven and Cloward, 1977).

Within the immigrant women's community, there is an increasing awareness of the problems of confining organizing efforts to state funded services. Further, constraints imposed by the state around legitimate forms of organization were raised for discussion by activists around the country, as evidenced by debates conducted in the Second National Conference on Immigrant and Visible Minority women (Winnipeg, November, 1986) and the Women and the State Conference

(Toronto, February, 1987). In particular, the class character of state-funded community services was discussed at length by immigrant women activists in the Women and the State Conference. Across the country, activists are confronting the divisiveness of state responses to immigrant women's demands (eg. through funding to selected community groups) and discussing new ways of challenging the state and its treatment of immigrant women.

Finally, I want to end by reflecting on my role as an analyst in relation to the community groups with whom I work. It is clear that the analyst is not in a position to "tell" a group what to do, or to develop a recipe for community struggle. This can only be done by the groups engaged in particular struggles themselves. In terms of my study on the employment agency, as an outsider I was in a better position to separate the structural problems (resulting from funding and other constraints) from the personal relations which became increasingly entwined as the story of the employment agency unfolded. As I see it, the analyst's responsibility is to make visible the structural constraints within which groups have to operate. In identifying existing sources of contradictions, the analyst can help groups to develop an ongoing analysis of new areas of struggles and change. In the above account, we saw that services provided by the state are not just means of social control; they also represent the battles fought and won by working people. At the same time, we saw how members of the agency participated in courses of action which led to their own oppression and to changes in the original intent of the agency. Ultimately, analyses of these contradictory processes enable us to discover how the state works to constrain and limit the actions of working people. More importantly, they can help us assess the strengths and weakness of various community actions and movements, so that we may work more effectively to transform the conditions of our lives.

# Notes

This book is based on my doctoral dissertation completed in September, 1984. In revising it for the Network Basic Series, I have omitted many technical details (eg. textual analyses of contracts and forms) and the literature review (eg. the theoretical debates on class, and a review of studies of immigrant women). The reader who seeks these details may turn to my dissertation, *Immigrant Women and the State: A Study in the Social Organization of Knowledge* [Department of Education (OISE), University of Toronto, 1984], for fuller discussions.

## CHAPTER 1

1. For fuller discussions of immigrant women in the labour force, see Arnopoulos (1979), Boyd (1975, 1986), Jenke and Yaron (1979), Ng and Das Gupta (1980, 1981), Ng and Ramirez (1981), Estable (1986).

2. For a long time, Marxist theorization of the state has been stuck in the "instrumentalist" versus the "structuralist" debate which centred around Miliband's refinement of and quarrel with the earlier works of Poulantzas. (For a summary of this debate, see Holloway and Picciotto, 1978.) Recently, the "state derivation" debate has gained popularity in Britain and western Europe (see Holloway and Picciotto, 1978; Jessop, 1982). I tend to agree with Poulantzas' suggestion in his later work that there can be no general theory of the state (Poulantzas, 1980). Although we can map out certain elements

of the capitalist state, a theory of the state has to undergo constant revision in accordance with the actual state of affairs and the particular configuration of class struggle in a social formation. Some of the usefulness of Poulantzas' later conceptualization has been critically assessed by Jessop (1982).

## CHAPTER 2

1. See, for example, the assessment criteria as outlined in an internal document entitled, "Ontario Region Outreach Program Strategy" dated November 29, 1978.

2. In this section, I am using the terms, "project" and "agency," to distinguish the two major phases of the development of the employment agency. "Project" refers to the phase prior to the incorporation process, when it was administered as an experimental project through another community organization. "Agency" refers to the phase after the incorporation process, when the project staff applied to the state to become legally constituted as a voluntary organization.

## CHAPTER 3

1. Ontario Region, Outreach Program Strategy, November 29, 1978, item (e) of "Assessment Factors."

2. Similarly, a review of the activities of the employment agency as outlined in the proposal, and those described in the agreement, indicates the way in which the activities of the agency were specified in enforceable and measurable terms:
   1. Activities described in the 1980-81 funding proposal to Outreach:
   i) *Job placement and referral*: contacting employers and setting up a large referral network of jobs suitable for immigrant women. This is a service helpful not only for the immigrant women but for employers seeking dependable help.
   ii) *Job orientation counselling*: to help clients get acquainted with the reality of the Canadian job market. For example, what jobs are available and the requirements of each kind of job. This is usually followed by self awareness exercises such as personal goal setting, estimate of one's values, motivations, personal skills, career objectives, with the understanding that they may have to choose from the alternatives that are available.
   iii) *Job search counselling*: the counsellors survey the needs and available openings in the area, thus providing the latter with guidelines for resume writing, filling out application forms, aptitude tests and job interviews.
   iv) Provide information, translation, escorting, advocacy and interpretation services connected with employment.

v) *Referral services*: to cooperate with other agencies that may help clients with their employment related needs (these are usually agencies that clients are reluctant to approach on their own—due to language barrier, ignorance of their services and other reasons). Some examples of these are referral to Manpower training programs, UIC, and day care arrangements.

vi) *Counselling services* for working immigrant women: to inform them of their rights such as unionization and benefits, obligations towards their employers, day care arrangements and how to fulfill the dual role of a mother and a career woman.

**2.** Activities as outlined in the contract between Outreach and the employment agency:

i) Job orientation counselling:
-providing information on the labour market, job requirements, training opportunities, labour legislation and regulations.

ii) Job search counselling:
-reviewing client needs and available employment opportunities,
-discussing alternative occupational goals,
-providing instruction on guidelines for resume writing, completing application forms, aptitude tests,
-providing exposure to employment interviews, work settings.

iii) Client marketing
-contacting employers and maintaining a large referral network of jobs suitable for immigrant women,
-referral of clients to sharing of job vacancies wih the CEC for further or additional service.

iv) Referral and placement of target group clientele in employment or training.

v) Provide clients with information on community, agency and various government services. Referral of clients to these services as required and cooperating with other agencies that can assist clients with employment-related needs (eg. U.I., Community and Social Services–Day Care Branch, Ministry of Culture & Recreation, etc.). Provide translation and interpretation services when required. Occasional escorting of clients.

vi) Maintain close liaison with district CEC. A plan of action is to be developed by 30 June 1980 by project and CEIC representatives to ensure that project clientele have the benefit of access to Commission programs and services such as institutional and industrial training (eg. CMIPT, CMPT, W.A.T.) testing.

vii) Document methods and procedures developed to resolve problems encountered, to ensure proper interpretation of target group clientele into the labour force. Detail these methods for CEIC on an ongoing basis so that CECS could become more competent to provide these services.

viii) In recognition of the fact that Outreach funds are limited, and are not available indefinitely, the project Board of Directors is empowered to pursue various channels for alternative funding to cover budget expenditures not assumed under Outreach.

ix) Project will submit regular financial, statistical, and narrative reports as required. Follow-up on clients registered will be performed on a regular basis.

x) Project will prominently display a sign indicating that funds are received from the CEIC. The Commissions contribution to supporting this service will also be mentioned in promotional and publicity material.

3. The division of work within the agency *vis-a-vis* EIC is as follows: The board of directors, notably the chairperson, were responsible for funding matters. They would deal directly with Outreach to negotiate for a new contract, or for an increment of funding for the current fiscal year, for example.

   The coordinator was responsible for the day-to-day administration of the agency, including the compilation and submission of various reports required by Outreach. She would answer inquiries by Employment and Immigration personnel about the agency's operation. Occasionally, if the inquiry pertained to the overall financial situation of the agency, she would refer the matter to the board.

   All members of the staff (i.e. the coordinator and other counsellors) could deal directly with CEC regarding matters concerning the clients of the agency. For instance, it would be quite appropriate for a counsellor to contact the CEC project officer about the placement of her client(s) in a training program sponsored by the Department of Employment and Immigration.

4. This was the case theoretically. In actual fact, many of the problems arising out of the placement of immigrant women into existing CEC programs were unresolvable because of the admission criteria established by these programs.

   For example, in order to obtain government subsidies for educational and training programs, Employment and Immigration required that the applicant be an independent immigrant (see Chapter One). Furthermore, many of the programs required a certain level of command of English, such as Grade 10 English or its equivalent, as a prerequisite. These programs automatically disqualified many immigrant women who were sponsored immigrants and who did not have the language proficiency enabling them to enroll.

   Since the majority of the agency's clients were non-English speaking women with little formal education, they could rarely be referred to these government programs. The agency was thus unable to demonstrate cooperation with the CECs through this kind of referral. Thus, an amiable working relationship with the CEC project officer became particularly important.

5. This information was obtained from the interview with the Outreach consultant in charge of the employment agency.

6. As I spent more time at the agency, I realized that the extent to which the

coordinator could prevent this kind of interference by Outreach was in fact minimal, since Outreach could easily hold back the monthly instalment of money to the agency. This was especially the case after an interim (4-month) contract was signed between Outreach and the employment agency for the 1981-82 fiscal year. The temporary nature of the agency's funding meant that members of the agency were more likely to succumb to pressure from the funding program.

7. This goes beyond "fudging" the statistics. The issue is that the breakdown of services into the EIC categories (eg. job search, employer contact) was meaningless in a face-to-face context with clients, where the counsellor carried out these activities simultaneously.

## CHAPTER 4

1. These objectives are: (a) To place immigrant women in meaningful employment and to help them with employment related needs; (b) To carry on the activities of a job placement, referral and counselling service and other activities as the need arises; and (c) To cooperate with other organizations which have object [sic] in whole or in part to the objectives of the Centre. (Article II of by-law)

2. Both the short-term goals and long-term objectives of the employment agency were spelt out clearly in its 1981 funding proposal to Outreach, as follows: "Due to the various barriers for immigrant women in the labour market, [the Centre] had no choice but to develop a service which addresses not only immediate short-term employment needs (i.e. finding jobs for immigrant women who need whatever job they can find) but also longer-term needs for upgrading skills, education and earning power."

3. The placement rate is calculated as follows: Total number of clients placed / total number of clients x 100%. During the 1980-81 fiscal year, the placement rate of the agency was 47%, compared with the rate of the CECs of around 10%.

## CHAPTER 5

1. In response to the agency's request for an increase in its 1981-82 budget, Outreach conducted an overall evaluation of the agency's performance. In addition to detailed statistical information on the aspects of the agency's operation, part of the evaluation process involved the visit by an evaluator to the agency to observe the counsellors' work. Needless to say, this incident put a great deal of stress on the already stressful climate of the agency at this time. I don't have much information on the evaluation because I was requested not to visit the agency during this time, a result of the fear that

using volunteer help would reflect negatively on the performance of the agency.

2. It is useful to remind the reader that the agency began as a breakaway group of another immigrant organization, the members of which indicated to the community that the organization was not serving the "real needs" of immigrant women. It is ironic that the agency itself had now come full circle to the same set of rationale put forward to the immigrant community in 1977.

3. While this is true, counsellors did try to accommodate clients from other groups. One way to serve the increasing Vietnamese clientele was to hire a counsellor who could speak both Chinese and Vietnamese. The problem in that case was that her caseload doubled as a result of this arrangement.

# Selected Bibliography


ARMSTRONG, Pat & ARMSTRONG, Hugh 1978 *The Double Ghetto: Canadian Women and their Segregated Work*. Toronto: McClelland and Stewart.

ARMSTRONG, Hugh 1977 "The Labour force and state workers in Canada" in Leo Panitch (ed), *The Canadian State: Political Economy and Political Power*. Toronto: University of Toronto Press.

ARNOPOULOUS, Sheila McLeod 1979 *Problems of Immigrant Women in the Canadian Labour Force*. Ottawa: Advisory Council on the Status of Women.

ASHWORTH, Mary 1976 "The settlement of immigrants: The need for a policy." Unpublished ms., Faculty of Education, UBC.

BASRAN, G.S. 1983 "Canadian immigration policy and theories of racism" in Peter S. Li and B. Singh Bolaria (eds), *Racial Minorities in Multicultural Canada*. Toronto: Garamond Press.

BENNETT, J.W. (ed) 1975 *The New Ethnicity: Perspectives from Ethnology*. New York: West Publishing.

BLAXALL, M. and REAGAN, B. (eds) 1976 *Women and the Workplace: The Implications of Occupational Segregation*. Chicago and London: University of Chicago Press.

BODNAR, Ana and REIMER, Marilee 1979 *The organization of social services and its immplications for the mental health of immigrant women*. Toronto: Working Women Community Centre.

BOULTER, Alison E. 1978 *Constituting ethnic difference: An ethnography of the Portuguese immigrant experience in Vancouver*. M.A. Thesis, Dept. of Anthropology and Sociology, UBC.

BOYD, Monica 1975 "The status of immigrant women in Canada" *Canadian Review of Sociology and Anthropology*, 12: 406-416.

BOYD, Monica 1986 "Immigrant women in Canada" in R.J. Simon and C.B. Brettell (eds), *International Migration. The Female Experience*. Totowa, N.J.: Rowman and Allanheld.

BRAVERMAN, Harry 1974 *Labor and Monopoly Capital. The Degradation of Work in the Twentieth Century*. New York: Monthly Review Press.

CAMPBELL, Marie L. 1980 "Sexism in British Columbia trade unions, 1900-1920" in C. Kess and B. Latham (eds), *In Her Own Right: Selected Essays on Women in B.C. History*. Victoria, B.C.: Camousun College.

CARCHEDI, G. 1977 *On the Economic Identification of Social Class*. London: NLB.

CASSIN, A. Marguerite and GRIFFITH, Alison I. 1981 "Class and ethnicity: Producing the difference that counts," *Canadian Ethnic Studies*, 8(1): 109-129.

CHUD, Rita and FORTES, Elizabeth 1974 *Immigrant Women in the Labour Force*. Vancouver Status of Women and the Vancouver YWCA.

COCKBURN, Cynthia 1977 *The Local State*. London: Pluto Press.

COCKBURN, Cynthia 1983 *Brothers: Male Dominance and Technological Change*. London: Pluto Press.

CONNELLY, Patricia 1979 *Last Hired, First Fired: Women and the Canadian Work Force*. Toronto: The Women's Press.

CORRIGAN, Paul and LEONARD, Peter 1978 *Social Work Practice Under Capitalism—A Marxist Approach*. London: MacMillan.

CORRIGAN, Philip and SAYER, Derek 1985 *The Great Arch—English State Formation and Cultural Revolution*. Oxford: Basil Blackwell.

DEHLI, Kari 1984 "Women in the community: Reform of schooling and motherhood in Toronto" Paper presented at the 1984 CSAA annual meeting.

DJAO, A.W. 1983 *Inequality and Social Policy. The Sociology of Social Welfare*. Toronto: John Wiley and Sons.

EDWARDS, John and BATLEY, Richard 1978 *The Politics of Positive Discrimination: An Evaluation of the Urban Programme, 1967-77*. London: Tavistock Publications.

EDWARDS, Richard 1979 *Contested Terrain—The Transformation of the Workplace in the Twentieth Century*. London: Heinemann.

ELLIOTT, Jean Leonard (ed) 1979 *Two Nations, Many Cultures: Ethnic Groups in Canada*. Scarborough: Prentice-Hall.

ELLIOTT, Jean L. 1979 "Canadian immigration: a historical assessment" in Jean Leonard Elliott (ed), *Two Nations, Many Cultures: Ethnic Groups in Canada*. Scarborough: Prentice-Hall.

ERICKSON, Frederick and SHULTZ, Jeffrey 1982 *The Counselor as Gatekeeper: Social Interaction in Interviews*. New York: Academic Press.

ESTABLE, Alma 1986 *Immigrant Women in Canada—Current Issues*. A Background Paper prepared for the Canadian Advisory Council for the Status of Women.

GANNAGÉ, Charlene 1986 *Double Day, Double Bind*. Toronto: Women's Press.

GRIFFITH, Alison 1979 "Who is an immigrant?" *Multiculturalism*, 2(4): 4-5.

HARTMANN, Heidi 1976 "Capitalism, patriarchy, and job segregation by sex" in M. Blaxall and B. Reagan (eds), *Women and the Workplace: The Implications of Occupational Segregation*. Chicago and London: University of Chicago Press.

HAWKINS, Freda 1970 *Women Immigrants in Canada*. A study prepared for the Royal Commission on the Status of Women.

HAWKINS, Freda 1972 *Canada and Immigration, Public Policy and Public Concern*. Montreal: McGill-Queen's University Press.

HOLLOWAY, John and PICCIOTTO, Sol (eds) *1978 State and Capital: A Marxist Debate*. London: Edward Arnold Publishers.

IMMIGRANT WOMEN OF SASKATCHEWAN (IWS) 1985 *Doubly Disadvantaged: The Women Who Immigrate to Canada*. Saskatoon: Author.

JACKSON, Nancy 1977 *Describing News: Toward an Alternative Account*. M.A. Thesis, Dept. of Anthropology and Sociology, UBC.

JACKSON, Nancy S. 1980 "Class relations and bureaucratic practice." Paper presented at the CSAA annual meeting, Montreal, June.

JANKE, Brenda and YARON, Ronny 1979 *A report on Conditions in the Labour Market and Training Opportunities for non-English Speaking Immigrant Women in Metro Toronto*. Toronto: Working Women Community Centre. October 1979.

JESSOP, Bob 1982 *The Capitalist State*. Oxford: Martin Robertson.

JOHNSON, Laura C. 1982 *The Seam Allowance: Industrial Home Sewing in Canada*. Toronto: Women's Educational Press.

JOHNSTON, W.A. 1980 "Marxism and social class: Recent Theory." Paper presented at the CSAA annual meeting, Montreal.

LATHAM, Barbara and KESS, Cathy (eds) 1980 *In Her Own Right: Selected Essays on Women's History in B.C.* Victoria, B.C.: Camousun College.

LAY, Jackie 1980 "To Columbia on the Tynemouth: The emigration of single women and girls in 1862" in Barbara Latham and Cathy Kess (eds), *In Her Own Right: Selected Essays on Women's History in B.C.* Victoria, B.C.: Camousun College.

LEPINE, Irene 1983 "Definitions of skill and labour shortages." Paper presented at the CSAA annual meeting, Vancouver, June.

LONDON-EDINBURGH WEEKEND RETURN GROUP 1979 *In and Against the State.* London: Pluto Press.

LONEY, Martin 1977 "A political ecomony of citizen participation" in Leo Panitch (ed), *The Canadian State: Political Economy and Political Power.* Toronto: University of Toronto Press.

MAO, Tse-tung 1967a "On practice" in *Selected Works of Mao Tse-tung, Vol 1.* Peking: Foreign Language Press.

MAO, Tse-tung 1967b "On contradiction" in *Selected Works of Mao Tse-tung, Vol 1.* Peking: Foreign Languages Press.

MARX, Karl 1954 *Capital, Volume 1.* Moscow: Progress Publishers.

MARX, Karl and ENGELS, F. 1967 *The Communist Manifesto.* Middlesex: Penguin Books.

MARX, Karl and ENGELS, F. 1970 *The German Ideology.* New York: International Publishers.

MILIBAND, Ralph 1969 *The State in Capitalist Society.* London: Quartet Books Ltd.

MILNER, Sheilagh Hodgins and MILNER, Henry 1973 *The Decolonization of Quebec.* Toronto: McClelland and Stewart.

MONTERO, Gloria 1977 *The Immigrants.* Toronto: James Lorimer and Co. Publishers.

MORGAN, Patricia 1981 "From battered wife to program client: the state's shaping of social problems," *Kapitalistate,* (9): 17-39.

MULLER, Jacob 1982 "Alinsky style community organization (ASCO): managing their neighbourhood for the local state." Paper presented at the WASA annual meeting, Saskatoon.

MULLER, Jacob 1984 "Management of urban neighbourhoods through radical community organizing: an illustration from Vancouver, Canada." Paper presented at the CSAA annual meeting, Guelph.

MULLER, Jacob 1987 "The soup kitchen: a critique of self-help," *Community Development Journal, 22(1): 36-45.*

NG, Roxana 1977 "The Vancouver Chinese immigrant community and social services," *RIKKA*, 4(3 & 4): 72-86.

NG, Roxana 1978 "The social relations of citizens participation in the Chinese community." Paper presented at the CSAA annual meeting, London, May.

NG, Roxana 1979a "Fieldwork as ideological practice." Paper presented at the CSAA annual meeting, Saskatoon, June.

NG, Roxana 1979b "Services for immigrant women: a critical analysis." Paper presented at the CSAA annual meeting, Saskatoon, June.

NG, Roxana 1980 "Locating class relations in ethnic experiences." Paper presented by invitation at the Canadian Ethnology Society, Montreal, February.

NG, Roxana 1981 "Constituting ethnic phenomenon: An account from the perspective of immigrant women," *Canadian Ethnic Studies*, 8(1) 97-108.

NG, Roxana 1982a "Sex, ethnicity, or class? Some methodological considerations." Paper presented at the British Sociological Association special meeting on *Gender and Society*, Manchester, England, April.

NG, Roxana 1982b "Immigrant women and the state: epistemological issues in participant observation." Paper presented by invitation at the Canadian Ethnological Society annual meeting, Vancouver, May.

NG, Roxana and DAS GUPTA, Tania 1980 "The captive labour force of non-English speaking immigrant women." Unpublished ms., Wollstonecraft Research Group, OISE, Toronto.

NG, Roxana and DAS GUPTA, Tania 1981 "Nation builders? The captive labour force of non-English speaking immigrant women," *Canadian Women's Studies*, 3(1): 83-89.

NG, Roxana, and RAMIREZ, Judith 1981 *Immigrant Housewives in Canada*. Toronto: Immigrant Women's Centre.

NG, R.; WALKER, G.; and MULLER, J. (eds) forthcoming *Community Organization and the Canadian State*. Toronto: Garamond Press.

PALMER, Howard (ed) 1975 *Immigration and the Rise of Multiculturalism*. Toronto: Copp Clark Publishing.

PANITCH, Leo (ed) 1977 *The Canadian State: Political Economy and Political Power*. Toronto: University of Toronto Press.

PEYROT, Mark 1982 "Caseload management: choosing suitable clients in a community health clinic agency," *Social Problems*, 30(2): 157-167.

PIVEN, Frances Fox and CLOWARD, Richard A. 1977 *Poor People's Movements: Why They Succeed, How they Fail*. New York: Vintage Books.

PORTER, John 1965 *The Vertical Mosaic: An Analysis of Social Class And Power in Canada*. Toronto: University of Toronto Press.

POULANTZAS, Nicos 1978 *Classes in Contemporary Capitalism*. London: Verso (originally published by NLB, 1974).

POULANTZAS, Nicos 1980 *State, Power, Socialism*. London: Verso (originally published by NLBH, 1978).

ROBBINS, E. 1975 "Ethnicity or class? Social relations in a small Canadian industrial community" in J.W. Bennett (ed), *The New Ethnicity: Perspectives from Ethnology*. New York: West Publishing.

ROBERTS, Barbara 1978 "A limited partnership: Canadian immigrationist reformers, big business, and the state, 1880-1920." Paper presented at the Berkshire Conference on Women's History, Mt. Holyoke Massachusetts, August.

ROBERTS, Barbara 1980 "Sex, politics and religion: Controversies in female immigration reform work in Montreal, 1881-1919," *Atlantis*, 6(1): 25-38, Fall.

SASSEN-KOOB, Saskia 1981 "Toward a conceptualization of immigrant labour," *Social Problems*, 29(1): 65-85.

SAYER, Derek 1979 *Marx's Method: Ideology, Science and Critique in Capital*. Sussex: The Harvester Press. 2nd printing, 1983.

SCHREADER, Alicia 1984 "The women's movement and the state: the political terrain of struggle." Unpublished research paper, School of Social Work, Carleton University.

SHERMAN, Julia and BECK, Evelyn (eds) 1979 *The Prism of Sex: Essays in the Sociology of Knowledge*. Wisconsin: University of Wisconsin Press.

SMITH, Dorothy E. 1974 "The social construction of documentary reality," *Sociological Inquiry*, 44(4): 257-268.

SMITH, Dorothy E. 1975a "What it might mean to do a Canadian sociology: The everyday world as problematic," *Canadian Journal of Sociology*, 1(3): 363-376.

SMITH, Dorothy E. 1975b "An analysis of ideological structures and how women are excluded: considerations for academic women," *Canadian Review of Sociology and Anthropology*, 12(4): 353-369.

SMITH, Dorothy E. 1978 "A peculiar eclipsing: Women's exclusion from man's culture," *Women's Studies International Quarterly*, 1: 281-295.

SMITH, Dorothy E. 1979 "A sociology for women" in Julia Sherman and Evelyn Beck (eds), *The Prism of Sex: Essays in the Sociology of Knowledge*. Wisconsin: University of Wisconsin Press.

SMITH, Dorothy E. 1981a "The experienced world as problematic: a feminist method." University of Saskatchewan, Sorokin Lectures, No. 12.

SMITH, Dorothy E. 1981b "On sociological description: A method from Marx," *Human Studies*, (4): 313-337.

SMITH, Dorothy E. 1981c "Institutional ethnography: a feminist method." Paper presented at the conference on the Political Economy of Gender Relations, OISE, Toronto. (An abbreviated version of the paper is published in *Resources For Feminist Research*, Vol. 16 No. 1, 1986.)

SMITH, Dorothy E. 1983 "Women, class and family" in Ralph Miliband and John Saville (eds), *The Socialist Register, 1983*. London: The Merlin Press. (Reprinted by Garamond Press, 1985.)

SMITH, Dorothy E. 1984 "Textually mediated organizations," *International Social Science Quarterly*, 36(1): 59-75.

SMITH, George forthcoming "Policing the Gay Community" in R. NG, G. WALKER, and J.MULLER (eds), *Community Organization and the Canadian State*. Toronto: Garamond Press.

STANDING COMMITTEE ON SOCIAL DEVELOPMENT 1982 Family Violence Study, Ontario. Transcript of morning sitting, Tuesday, July 20, 1982.

STANLEY, Liz and WISE, Sue 1983 *Breaking Out: Feminist Consciousness and Feminist Research*. London: Routledge and Kegan Paul.

THERBORN, Göran 1980 *What Does the Ruling Class Do When it Rules? State Apparatuses and State Power under Feudalism, Capitalism and Socialism*. London: Verso.

THOMPSON, E.P. 1963 *The Making of the English Working Class*. Middlesex: Penguin.

VAN DEN BERGHE, Pierre 1975 "Ethnicity and class in Highland Peru" in L. Depres (ed), *Ethnicity and Resource Competition in Plural Societies*. The Hague: Mouton Publishers.

WHEELER, Stanton (ed) 1969 *On Record: Files and Dossiers in American Life*. New York: Russell Sage Foundation.

WILLIAMS, Raymond 1961 *Culture and Society*. Middlesex: Penguin.

WILLIS, Paul 1977 *Learning to Labour: How Working Class Kids Get Working Class Jobs*. Farnborough: Saxon House.

WRIGHT, E.O. 1976 "Class boundaries in advanced capitalist societies," *New Left Review*, 98: 3-41.

ZIMMERMAN, Don H. 1969 "Record-keeping and the intake process in a public welfare agency" in Stanton Wheeler (ed), *On Record: Files and Dossiers in American Life*. New York: Russell Sage Foundation.

ZIMMERMAN, Don H. 1974 "Fact as a practical accomplishment" in Roy Turner (ed), *Ethnomethodology*. Middlesex: Penguin.

## Garamond Books:

- Argue, Gannagé, Livingstone: *Working People and Hard Times: Canadian Perspectives*
- Basran and Hay: *Political Economy of Agriculture in Western Canada*
- Bolaria and Li (eds): *Racial Oppression in Canada* (2nd. ed.)
- Brickey and Comack (eds): *The Social Basis of Law*
- Brym (ed): *The Structure of the Canadian Capitalist Class*
- Burrill and McKay: *People, Resources and Power*
- Cantelon and Hollands: *Leisure, Sport and Working Class Cultures*
- Centennial College English Faculty Association: *Writing for the Job*
- Dickinson and Russell: *Family, Economy and State*
- Gruneau: *Popular Cultures and Political Practices*
- Henderson: *The Future on the Table*
- Knuttila: *State Theories: From Liberalism to the Challenge of Feminism*
- Livingstone (ed): *Critical Pedagogy & Cultural Power*
- Moscovitch and Albert (eds): *The Benevolent State: The Growth of the Welfare State*
- Niosi: *Canadian Multinationals*
- Olsen: *Industrial Change and Labour Adjustment in Sweden and Canada*
- Panitch & Swartz: *From Consent to Coercion* (2nd. ed.)
- Young (ed): *Breaking the Mosaic: Ethnic Identities in Canadian Schooling*

**The Network Basic Series**

- Acheson, Frank and Frost: *Industrialization and Underdevelopment in the Maritimes, 1880-1930*
- Armstrong and Armstrong: *Theorizing Women's Work*
- Armstrong et al: *Feminist Marxism or Marxist Feminism*
- Buchbinder et al: *Who's On Top: The Politics of Heterosexuality*
- Burstyn and Smith: *Women, Class, Family and the State*; Intro by Ng
- Cohen: *Free Trade and the Future of Women's Work*
- Duffy, Mandell and Pupo: *Few Choices: Women, Work and Home*
- Lacombe: *Ideology and Public Policy: The Case Against Pornography*
- Livingstone: *Social Crisis and Schooling*
- Lowe and Northcott: *Under Pressure: a Study of Job Stress*
- Luxton and Rosenberg: *Through the Kitchen Window: the Politics of Home and Family*
- Newson and Buchbinder: *The University Means Business*
- Ng: *The Politics of Community Services*
- Veltmeyer: *The Canadian Class Structure*
- Veltmeyer: *Canadian Corporate Power*
- White: *Law, Capitalism and the Right to Work*

Garamond Press, 67A Portland St., Toronto, Ont., M5V 2M9
(416) 597-0246